FROM FAMILY SCAPEGOAT
TO SUMMIT

FROM FAMILY SCAPEGOAT TO SUMMIT

SHEDDING LABELS AND PAVING YOUR LEGACY

EMILY CLARK

REPRYRNTED

CONTENTS

FREE GIFT

To assist you on your healing journey, I've crafted this FREE companion resource to the book.

You can get instant access to **The Scapegoat's Workbook** by either clicking the link or scanning the QR code below.

This bonus is 100% free with no strings attached. You don't need to provide any personal information except your email address (so that I can send it to you).

This interactive workbook allows you to put the theory into practice and tailor your recovery strategies to your specific experiences and situations.

To get your bonus, go to:

subscribe.reprynted.com/family-scapegoat-bonus

Or scan the QR code below

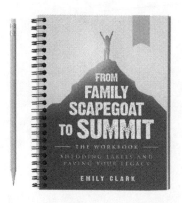

This **workbook** and **journal** is designed as a companion to the main book. It provides you with practical exercises, reflective prompts, and guided journaling sections tailored to each chapter of the book. This **interactive resource** aims to further facilitate the healing process by allowing you to actively engage with the material, reflect on your personal experiences, and track your progress over time.

Personalized Journey: The workbook allows you to customize your healing journey, ensuring that your unique experiences and feelings are addressed.

Practical Application: It translates the theoretical and informational content of the book into actionable steps, ensuring that you can apply what you learn.

Progress Tracking: By regularly journaling and completing exercises, you can visibly see your progress, reinforcing motivation and commitment to recovery.

INTRODUCTION
THE GENESIS OF SCAPEGOATING

> In every family, there's a story that defines its history. But sometimes, there's also a label that attempts to define its members.

As I sat cross-legged on my favorite antique rug during a meditative retreat in Nepal, I was flooded with memories from my past - memories of laughter, love, challenges, and disappointments. But the ones that clung to me most tenaciously were those intertwined with a label that was thrust upon me, a title I never asked for nor deserved. That label was the 'scapegoat.'

This title, as weighty as the mountains that surrounded me, had cast a shadow over much of my early life, as it does for countless others. While labels can be peeled off jars and bottles, the labels affixed to our souls are much more tenacious. This journey of understanding and freeing oneself from such labels isn't just about shedding a title; it's about a profound transformation, akin to the metamorphosis of a caterpillar into a butterfly.

For every individual who's been pinned down by labels, especially that of the family scapegoat, this is your sanctuary. Your place of understanding. Your path to liberation. Let's embark on this transformative journey together, shedding the weight of undeserved labels and soaring to new heights of self-discovery.

The term 'scapegoat' finds its origins in ancient rituals. Picture this: an ancient community standing together, collectively pouring their sins, mistakes, and regrets onto an innocent goat, then sending it into the wilderness, hoping to be absolved of their misdeeds. This goat bore the weight of an entire community's transgressions, bearing a burden it never created.

Translating this to the modern context, especially within the intricacies of family dynamics, the scapegoat's role isn't much different. Within the family structure, the scapegoat becomes the chosen one – the individual who, often unintentionally, bears the blame for the family's shortcomings, dysfunctions, and unresolved tensions. It's as if the family collectively projects their imperfections onto this member, hoping, perhaps subconsciously, to maintain a facade of normalcy or perfection for the outside world.

This role, as you can imagine, comes with a slew of negative connotations. The scapegoat often feels isolated, misunderstood, and perennially at fault, even when logic dictates otherwise. They're the 'black sheep', the 'troublemaker', or the 'difficult one', never quite fitting into the family's narrative of what they should be. The emotional burden is palpable, like wearing a heavy, sodden cloak that refuses to dry.

But why is there a scapegoat in many families? The reasons can be manifold. Some families need a diversion from their internal problems. Others might be unconsciously continuing a pattern that has been handed down for generations. Then there are those families where the balance of power is so skewed that one member becomes an easy target for the rest.

Understanding this role is essential not just for the scapegoat, but for every member of the family. Recognizing this dynamic can be the first step toward healing, reconciliation, and building a healthier family system where every individual is acknowledged and valued for who they truly are, not just the role they've been cast into.

It's a subtle undertow in the sea of family dynamics - that creeping feeling of constantly being in the wrong, of standing out, not for your achievements or unique qualities, but for being the perennial problem child. The family scapegoat, while living amid the familiar surroundings of kin, often feels like an outsider peering into a world where they don't quite belong.

Why, you might wonder, is it so pivotal to recognize when you're wearing this uncomfortable badge? Well, imagine navigating a maze blindfolded. That's what living in oblivion of the scapegoat role feels like. You bump into walls of misunderstanding, trip over stones of blame, and get tangled in the thorny bushes of unmet expectations. Recognizing that you're in this maze is the first, and perhaps the most crucial step, towards finding your way out.

The scapegoat label isn't just a familial tag; it becomes an identity. It shapes how you view yourself, how you interact with the world, and sadly, how you value your worth. Living under this shadow can cloud your perception, making you question your every move, doubt your every decision, and filter your experiences through a lens of inherent guilt.

Yet, with recognition comes clarity. Once you discern the patterns, the repeated cycles of blame and shame, you can begin to challenge them. You start to see that it's not about you; it's about a dysfunctional dynamic that you've been inadvertently pulled into.

And here's the empowering part: with recognition comes the possibility of change. By understanding your role, you reclaim the narrative of your life. You can choose to rewrite your story, not as the black sheep, but as the resilient survivor, the introspective seeker, the authentic self that's been overshadowed for far too long.

Recognition is akin to that first breath after being underwater for too long. It's refreshing, illuminating, and absolutely essential. It paves the way for healing, for breaking the chains that have held you back, and most importantly, for reclaiming the vibrant, authentic self that lies beneath the weighty cloak of the scapegoat.

Ah, the life of a scapegoat. It isn't just a series of undeserved accusations or the brunt of misplaced blame. It's akin to carrying a backpack, constantly being filled with the family's emotional clutter, heavy with resentment, unresolved conflicts, and unspoken pain. That backpack isn't just metaphoric; it takes its toll on the very essence of who you are, shaping your psyche, emotional well-being, and even, in some cases, your physical health.

Emotionally, imagine constantly walking on eggshells, never quite sure of which misstep will spark the next round of blame. It breeds a cocktail of volatile feelings: frustration from being misunderstood, anger at the unjust accusations, sadness from the lack of genuine connection, and often, an underlying layer of anxiety, always waiting for the other shoe to drop. There's an ever-present cloud of self-doubt, often manifesting as the nagging voice that wonders if, maybe, you really are the problem.

Mentally, this role can lead to a distorted self-image. If you're constantly viewed through a lens of fault, you might start believing you're inherently flawed. It could manifest as debilitating perfectionism, where you're always trying to prove yourself, or perhaps a defeatist attitude, resigning yourself to the 'fact' that you'll never be good enough. The mental gymnastics of navigating family dynamics can also birth coping mechanisms like denial, disassociation, or even self-sabotaging behaviors.

Physically? Chronic stress, which many scapegoats experience, isn't just an emotional challenge. It has tangible effects on the body. From sleep disturbances, chronic fatigue, to a weakened immune system or even stress-induced ailments like headaches or digestive issues. Our bodies often bear the brunt of our emotional battles, translating psychological pain into physical symptoms.

And here's a little teaser: while this might paint a grim picture, it's essential to understand the depth of these effects to fully appreciate the transformative journey of healing, growth, and empowerment that awaits. So, as we dive into the upcoming chapters, brace yourself for an exploration not just of the challenges, but of the myriad ways to rise above them. Because, dear reader, while being the scapegoat might shape parts of your narrative, it doesn't define your entire story.

Growing up, my family home was a lovely place filled with the typical sounds of life – laughter, heated discussions, playful banter, and sometimes, the shattering of a vase. No, that wasn't a metaphor. I'm talking about an actual vase.

On one fateful day, as the youngest of four siblings, I bounded into our living room after school, a bounce in my step, eager to recount my adventures on the playground. That enthusiasm was halted when I found the family gathered around the remnants of a treasured family heirloom vase, faces fraught with a mix of sadness and anger.

Without missing a beat, all eyes turned to me. My older brother, with an exaggerated sigh, said, "Emily, were you playing ball in the house again?"

The truth? I hadn't even seen the broken vase until that very moment. But a chorus of agreement rang out, weaving a narrative of my supposed carelessness. Confused and taken aback, I stammered out my denials, but they fell on deaf ears. It was as if I had a label stamped on my forehead: "The Clumsy One" or more aptly, "The Convenient One to Blame."

Instances like these weren't isolated events. If a cookie went missing, if the TV remote disappeared, if someone's diary was touched (I'm looking at you, middle sister), I was the prime suspect. The role of family scapegoat was, it seemed, my birthright as the youngest child.

The weight of those labels was crushing. Over time, I internalized them, genuinely believing that perhaps I was the problem, that I was inherently flawed. When things went wrong, even outside of home, I'd catch myself thinking, "Is it my fault?" My confidence wavered, friendships strained, and I often found myself isolated, too afraid to speak up or take up space, lest I be blamed for something else.

This story isn't a bid for sympathy. No, it's a reflection of a deeper truth – that sometimes, families, bound by love, complexities, and unresolved dynamics, inadvertently cast one of their own into a role that isn't rightfully theirs. It's about the confusion, the hurt, the feeling of being perpetually "lost in labels."

I share this because I know I'm not alone. For anyone who's felt misunderstood, sidelined, or boxed into a role they never auditioned for, this tale might resonate. And while these stories form part of our history, they don't have to dictate our future.

The stories we're told, the roles we're given, and the labels we wear can shape our identity, sometimes in ways that don't truly reflect who we are. This book is about discovering that misalignment and daring to rewrite our narratives.

"From Family Scapegoat to Summit: Shedding Labels and Paving Your Legacy" is not just a collection of insights or a mere guide. It's an empowering journey that I invite you on, one where you'll uncover, confront, and ultimately shed the ill-fitting roles you've been assigned in your family. It's for those who've felt the sting of undeserved blame, the weight of unwarranted shame, and the isolation that comes from being misunderstood.

The purpose of this tome is threefold:

1. Recognition: Before we can change our story, we must first recognize the role we've been unwittingly playing. This book will guide you in identifying the signs and dynamics that cast you as the family scapegoat.

2. Healing: Knowledge, while powerful, is just the beginning. Understanding our pain is one thing; healing from it is another. Through therapeutic insights, practical exercises, and stories of hope, we'll embark on a transformative journey from hurt to healing.

3. Reclamation: Beyond healing is the reclaiming of one's identity, power, and voice. By the end of this book, you won't only break free from the limiting labels of the past but also pave a path for a brighter, self-defined future.

Whether you're reading this book out of curiosity, for a loved one, or because you suspect or know that you've been the family scapegoat, my hope is that these pages offer solace, understanding, and actionable steps towards a more authentic life.

Together, let's step out of the shadows of misconception and into the light of our true selves.

The journey you're embarking upon, dear reader, is not for the faint-hearted. It demands introspection, courage, and a will to confront some of life's harshest truths. But like any formidable mountain's summit, the view from the top—the freedom, clarity, and self-affirmation—is unparalleled and worth every strenuous step.

Breaking free from the suffocating embrace of the scapegoat label is about more than just liberating oneself from undue blame. It's about reclaiming your narrative, understanding your worth, and laying down bricks for a legacy built on authenticity and strength, not on others' misperceptions.

This introduction serves as a compass, pointing you in the direction of understanding and self-realization. But the chapters that follow? They're your roadmap, replete with insights, personal tales, and practical tools, leading you out of the maze of misjudgment and into the open fields of self-acceptance.

So, as we transition from understanding the concept to diving deep into the dynamics, strategies, and healing processes, I hope you carry with you a sense of hope and determination. Remember, every story can be rewritten, every label can be shed, and every soul can find its summit.

Continue with me. Let's journey from the valleys of misconception to the peaks of self-realization, hand in hand.

1

UNRAVELING THE DYNAMICS
THE ROOTS AND REASONS

The aroma of roasted meat wafted through the small alleyways of my childhood home, a nostalgic scent that instantly took me back to Sunday family dinners. While many families gather around the table in joy, ours was a mixture of laughter, love, and, unfortunately, blame. I remember the weight of invisible fingers always pointing at me. In those moments, I was their scapegoat, the convenient receptacle for frustrations, mistakes, and unspoken grievances. But why me? Why was I, Emily Clark, the chosen one for this role?

Welcome, dear reader, to a journey that dives deep into the labyrinthine corridors of family dynamics, shedding light on the shadows cast by the age-old practice of scapegoating. The practice's historical roots stretch back to ancient times, weaving through various cultures and epochs. It isn't merely a familial issue; it has broader societal implications. To understand the scapegoat's role in modern family units, we must first journey back in time, across cultures, to uncover the phenomenon's multi-faceted origins.

The scapegoat phenomenon isn't confined to a particular era or geography. From the crowded streets of ancient Jerusalem to the vast expanse of the African savannahs, scapegoating has been a societal constant, evolving over time and adapting to its surroundings. As we set the stage for a deeper exploration, it's crucial to appreciate the pervasive nature of this practice and its intricate connection with our shared human experience.

By understanding its origins and nuances, you're not just gaining knowledge; you're arming yourself with the tools to break free. You're no longer just a pawn in a complex game; you're reclaiming the narrative. So, as we embark on this journey together, I encourage you to keep an open mind and heart. Allow the stories of yesteryears to illuminate your path, helping you see your role in a new light.

As we unravel these dynamics, remember this: you are not alone. Many have walked this path before, and together, we'll chart a course towards understanding, healing, and, ultimately, liberation.

Ever wondered about the odd sensation of being blamed for something you didn't do? That unsettling feeling in the pit of your stomach when accusations fly your way, with no basis in reality? Welcome to the intricate web of scapegoating.

Imagine a world where mistakes and misdeeds needed an outlet, a receptacle, where all could direct their anger, frustration, and guilt. Scapegoating is precisely that - a psychological mechanism that redirects blame, responsibility, and negative feelings away from oneself or a collective and onto another individual or group. It's like an emotional "hot potato" game, where no one wants to hold onto the negative energy or accountability, so they pass it on. But unlike the game, the scapegoat doesn't willingly choose to be "it."

While the broader definition of scapegoating can span various arenas, from politics to workplaces, within the family unit, it takes on an even more intimate and potent dimension. Families, being our primary social units, are expected to be our safe havens. Yet, paradoxically, they can sometimes become the breeding grounds for patterns of blame and unfair treatment. In these close-knit environments, one member (often perceived as the weakest or most vulnerable) becomes the chosen one to bear the burdens of the collective. This "chosen one" absorbs the negative feelings, the disappointments, and the unresolved traumas of the family, often without understanding why.

Why does this happen? The family might be attempting to maintain a semblance of normalcy or coherence. By projecting their collective failures or anxieties onto one member, the rest can maintain an illusion of functionality or even superiority. It's easier to point a finger at one person and say, "It's because of them!" than to introspect and address underlying issues.

But let's be clear. The scapegoat is often innocent, merely a convenient vessel for the projected emotions of others. They might even internalize this blame, believing they are genuinely at fault, eroding their self-esteem and skewing their self-perception. The injustice of it all is palpable, but to truly grasp its depth, we must understand it in relation to other family roles and explore its historical and cultural roots.

Navigating a family's complex dynamics often feels akin to acting on a stage. Each family member plays a role, cast either by themselves or by others, with distinct characteristics and scripts. While the scapegoat might be the most discussed role in this book, it's vital to recognize that it doesn't exist in isolation. The roles intermingle and interact, creating a captivating, often tumultuous, family drama.

The Scapegoat: As we've delved into, the scapegoat is the "fall guy," absorbing blame, shame, and the family's collective discontents. They're frequently the disruptors, the ones who call out the family's dysfunction, hence becoming convenient targets for blame. Ironically, they often possess the strength to face the family's underlying issues, even if they're unjustly punished for it.

The Hero: Often seen as the golden child or the family's pride bearer, the hero is perceived as the "perfect one." They achieve, they excel, and they often take on responsibilities beyond their age. The pressure on the hero can be immense, and while they might enjoy accolades and positive attention, they may also feel trapped in their role, afraid to fail or show vulnerability. Their achievements, while laudable, can serve as a smokescreen, deflecting attention from the family's deeper issues.

The Mascot: The mascot is the family's clown or the tension diffuser. They use humor as a coping mechanism, often lightening up intense situations. While they bring laughter and relief to the family setting, this role can mask their own pain or anxieties. They might feel an implicit expectation to always be jovial, overshadowing their authentic feelings and needs.

The Lost Child: Quiet and reticent, the lost child avoids drawing attention, often retreating into their own world.

They may bury themselves in books, art, or fantasy worlds. They're the peacemakers, choosing isolation or invisibility over conflict. Their withdrawal, however, is a silent scream, a way to cope in a chaotic environment without adding to it.

Each family member, knowingly or unknowingly, dons one of these roles, or sometimes even oscillates between them. These roles are not stagnant; they can shift based on evolving family dynamics. What's critical to understand is that each role is a coping strategy, an adaptation to the family's unique environment. While some roles might seem more desirable or easier than others, each comes with its own set of challenges and burdens.

It's like a dance, choreographed over time. The hero shines, the mascot jokes, the lost child fades, and the scapegoat rebels or hurts – all in response to each other and the larger family narrative. The interplay can be harmonious or discordant, but each member contributes to the family's song, its underlying rhythms, and beats.

The word "scapegoat" conjures up modern images of blame and unfairness, but to truly understand its depth, we need to venture back in time, tracing its origins to ancient rituals and biblical texts.

The term "scapegoat" has its roots in the Hebrew Bible, specifically in the Book of Leviticus. The ancient Israelites practiced a ritual on Yom Kippur, the Day of Atonement, which was their most solemn and significant holy day. On this day, two goats were chosen: one to be sacrificed to the Lord and another to be sent away into the wilderness, bearing the sins of the community.

The high priest would lay his hands upon the head of this latter goat, symbolically transferring the sins of the people onto it. This act of transference was a powerful visual representation of the community's sins being taken away. The goat, now bearing these transgressions, was led into the desert and set free, symbolically carrying away the sins with it. In Hebrew, this goat was referred to as the "Azazel," which, over time and through linguistic evolution, was translated into the English term "scapegoat."

This ancient ritual was not just about sin transference but also about purification and renewal. It allowed the community a fresh start, unburdened by the weight of their transgressions. The scapegoat, though bearing no guilt of its own, served as a vessel for the collective wrongs of the people.

Over centuries, the term "scapegoat" evolved from this specific religious rite to a more generalized notion of an individual or group unjustly blamed for the wrongdoings or misfortunes of others. While the exact practices and religious connotations faded, the concept persisted, finding its place in various cultures, societies, and situations. From political arenas to school playgrounds, and yes, to family living rooms, the act of scapegoating became a universal phenomenon, a mechanism to externalize blame and avoid personal or collective responsibility.

The power of the scapegoat narrative lies not just in its historical and religious significance but in its continued resonance in modern contexts. It serves as a stark reminder of humanity's propensity to shift blame, to find an "other" to carry our collective burdens, even when undeserving.

It's fascinating to realize that while scapegoating as a term finds its roots in ancient Hebrew traditions, the act itself, the psychological mechanism of offloading blame onto an innocent party, is not confined to any one culture or epoch. This phenomenon transcends geographical borders and historical timelines, manifesting in various traditions, rituals, and stories across the world.

Greek Mythology: Perhaps one of the most vivid tales of scapegoating comes from ancient Greece. Think of Prometheus, who stole fire from the gods to give to humans. For his transgression, he was chained to a rock and had an eagle feast on his liver daily. While he acted for the betterment of humanity, he bore the punishment alone, symbolizing the one who takes on the collective blame for the broader good.

African Cultures: In some African traditions, animals were used to bear the collective sins or misdeeds of a community. A ritual might involve villagers touching or hitting the animal, thereby transferring their wrongs, after which the animal would be released or sacrificed, paralleling the ancient scapegoat ritual.

Japanese Folklore: The Noppera-bō are faceless creatures found in Japanese tales. These beings often reflected societal fears about anonymity and the loss of identity, indirectly pointing towards the act of scapegoating. By assigning blame to faceless entities, one could avoid personal responsibility, similar to how scapegoats function in family dynamics.

Native American Cultures: Certain tribes practiced rituals wherein an individual would willingly take on the role of the 'sin-eater.' They'd perform dances or rites absorbing the wrongdoings of others, thereby purifying the tribe. This individual, while respected for their sacrifice, often lived on the fringes of society, bearing the weight of the collective guilt.

India: The concept of Karma in Hindu philosophy can sometimes lead to scapegoating. If someone suffers misfortune, it's often attributed to their past life's deeds, which not only shifts blame but also reinforces social hierarchies and legitimizes mistreatment.

European History: Witch hunts during the Middle Ages and Renaissance periods in Europe offer a bleak view into scapegoating. Women, often those marginalized or different, were blamed for societal ills, bad harvests, or diseases. They became the scapegoats, persecuted for the broader community's misfortunes.

These examples, though from diverse backgrounds and timelines, underscore a shared human tendency: the need to externalize blame, to find an "other" upon which we can project our fears, insecurities, and wrongdoings. It speaks to a universal theme, one of deflection and avoidance, illuminating why scapegoating remains relevant even in contemporary times. The cultural garments may vary, but the essence of scapegoating remains remarkably consistent.

The narrative of scapegoating is as ancient as storytelling itself, a thread woven through the fabric of time. But like all tales that endure, it has evolved, shifting shapes and shades to mirror the world it exists within.

Ancient Ritualistic Beginnings: As we've discussed, early manifestations of scapegoating were deeply ritualistic. Whether in the form of the Hebrew ceremony or the African tribes releasing a marked animal, these rites served a dual purpose. They aimed at both external cleansing – ridding the community of tangible evils or wrongdoings – and internal catharsis – a symbolic release of guilt or anxiety.

Medieval to Renaissance Transition: Fast-forward a few centuries, and we find scapegoating taking on darker, more malignant forms. The European witch hunts stand as a stark reminder. Here, the act wasn't just symbolic; it had dire, often fatal consequences for the scapegoats. This evolution, from symbolic to actual persecution, underscored societal shifts—growing fears of the unknown, religious upheavals, and power struggles.

Modern Psychological Manifestations: As societies became more complex, so did the reasons for scapegoating. It began to seep into the collective psyche. In families, especially dysfunctional ones, it became a coping mechanism. Instead of addressing core issues like financial stresses, marital discord, or mental health challenges, it was easier to offload these anxieties onto one member, turning them into the proverbial black sheep.

What's especially intriguing in the modern context is the subtlety. Unlike the overt rituals of yore, modern scapegoating in families can be insidious. It's in the offhand remarks, the not-so-subtle blames, the silent treatment after a family dispute. And because it's less overt, it often goes unrecognized, with the scapegoat internalizing this blame, leading to a host of psychological challenges.

From Societal to Personal: Earlier, scapegoating often served to address societal or community anxieties. Today, while it still exists in broader societal structures (think of minority groups being blamed for economic downturns), its more frequent manifestation is personal and familial. It's become a tool to navigate the intimate complexities of family dynamics, making it both more personal and more damaging.

The Role of Media and Digital Age: With the rise of digital media, scapegoating has found new platforms. Social media, for instance, often amplifies this behavior. A public figure makes a mistake, and they are instantly vilified, bearing the brunt of collective anger and frustrations.

As we journey from the dusty roads of ancient rituals to the digital highways of today, one thing remains constant: the human need to deflect blame. But with understanding comes the power of change. Recognizing this pattern, especially in intimate settings like the family, is the first step towards healing. And that, dear reader, is the journey we're on.

The tapestry of family is intricate and interwoven, with each thread representing a relationship, a history, and a dynamic. Sometimes, amid the colorful patchwork of laughter, love, and memories, there are shadows—shadows of dysfunction and distortion. It is within these shaded regions that the scapegoat often emerges.

Broken Communication: One of the most discernible patterns that birth the role of the scapegoat is fractured communication. Families that struggle to express feelings, concerns, or grievances openly tend to foster environments where internalized frustrations find an external outlet. Instead of addressing the root cause—be it jealousy between siblings or discontentment between partners—these feelings get redirected towards a convenient target, often someone seen as vulnerable or different.

Unresolved Traumas: A family's past can haunt its present. Unresolved traumas, whether they stem from events like abuse, loss, or betrayals, often cascade down generations. Instead of addressing the pain and healing collectively, some families find it easier to assign blame. The scapegoat becomes a vessel, bearing the burden of these traumas, even if they were not directly involved in the original events.

Power Imbalances: Hierarchies are not just corporate ladders; they exist within the household too. Often, these are based on age, gender, or even economic contributions. Those in dominant positions, intentionally or otherwise, may suppress or dominate others. When someone challenges this power structure or doesn't fit neatly into it, they may be relegated to the scapegoat role. The unspoken rule becomes clear: maintain the status quo, or face ostracization.

Differences and Deviations: In families that value uniformity—whether in beliefs, ambitions, or lifestyles—any deviation becomes noticeable. A child who dreams differently, a teenager who rebels, or a family member who comes out as LGBTQ+ might inadvertently challenge the family's perceived norms. These individuals, by merely being themselves, might get painted as the 'problem,' when in fact they are just revealing the underlying rigidity of the family structure.

The Role of External Influences: Sometimes, it's not just what's happening inside the family but outside that

drives the scapegoating. Societal norms, pressures, or prejudices can seep in, dictating how a family 'should' function.
For instance, families might face external economic pressures, leading to heightened internal tensions. Instead of
banding together, they might find it easier to blame a
member who isn't 'contributing enough,' even if the reasons
for their situation are entirely beyond their control.

The alchemy that turns a family member into a scapegoat
isn't a singular event but a culmination of dynamics, histories, and patterns. By recognizing these elements, families
can start the challenging yet rewarding journey of breaking
the cycle and healing together.

In the intricate dance of familial relationships, distractions
often play a pivotal role, especially when confronting the
reality becomes too daunting. The scapegoat, in many situations, becomes a diversion, a smokescreen that shields the
family from the pressing issues lurking beneath the surface.
Financial strains, marital discord, external societal pressures, or even the haunting specter of past mistakes can
fester, creating an atmosphere thick with tension. Rather
than addressing these volatile matters head-on, which
would require introspection, accountability, and change,
families might find it easier to divert attention towards a
scapegoat. This individual becomes the focal point of frustrations and blame, even if unrelated to the actual issues at
hand. In a way, by concentrating negativity onto one
member, the family creates an illusion of unity against a
common 'problem,' allowing them to momentarily evade the
more profound, more uncomfortable truths that threaten to
disrupt the family equilibrium. The tragedy of this
dynamic is that while the scapegoat bears an undue burden,
the real issues remain unresolved, often leading to a cycle of

pain that affects every family member, directly or indirectly.

The intricate web of family dynamics, with all its unspoken rules, emotional histories, and hidden insecurities, is governed by a host of psychological mechanisms. Often, these mechanisms play a key role in determining which family member assumes the scapegoat mantle. Let's delve into some of these factors:

Birth Order: The position one holds in the sequence of siblings can have profound implications. For instance, first-born children, often viewed as the standard bearers and expected to be the role models, might sometimes be scapegoated when they fail to meet high expectations. Conversely, the youngest might be scapegoated because they're seen as the "baby" and potentially more vulnerable or less capable of defending themselves. Middle children, sometimes feeling overlooked, might also be scapegoated as they may not have a clearly defined 'role' like their siblings.

Personality Traits: Personality plays a pivotal role in these dynamics. A child who is more sensitive, introverted, or questioning might stand out in a family that values toughness, extroversion, or conformity. Such a child could easily become a scapegoat, especially if the family sees these traits as 'problems' needing fixing. Similarly, a fiercely independent child in a tightly-knit, conformist family might become the focal point of blame simply because they challenge the status quo.

Deviations from Family Norms: In families with rigid norms and values, any deviation, be it in terms of beliefs, sexuality, career choices, or even lifestyle, can lead to scapegoating. For example, a child who chooses a career in arts in a family of lawyers and doctors might be viewed as the 'black sheep'. Or, in more conservative households, a member coming out as LGBTQ+ might sadly be cast into the scapegoat role, bearing the brunt of the family's prejudices and fears.

Underlying Psychological Issues: Sometimes, the scapegoating might not just be about the scapegoat's traits but more about the issues of those doing the scapegoating. Parents or siblings with unresolved traumas, personality disorders, or other mental health challenges might project their insecurities, fears, and unresolved issues onto a family member, creating a scapegoat in the process.

In essence, the act of scapegoating is rarely a reflection of the individual being targeted. Instead, it mirrors the complexities, insecurities, and unresolved issues within the family unit. Recognizing this is a crucial step towards healing, not just for the scapegoat, but for the entire family.

Scapegoating, while a term with ancient origins, still permeates the modern tapestry of family dynamics with an unsettling tenacity. This chapter has illuminated the multifaceted nature of the scapegoat phenomenon, from its historical and cultural depths to its roots in our personal family narratives. We've delved into the core reasons why certain individuals find themselves unwittingly wearing the heavy mantle of the family scapegoat, a title that carries the burden of blame, distraction, and dysfunction.

As we've uncovered, scapegoating is not just an isolated event, but rather a complex interplay of psychology, family dynamics, and societal influences. Recognizing this pattern is the first step to healing. However, knowledge alone isn't enough; it's merely the foundation upon which one can begin the journey of self-reclamation.

The road to understanding, while enlightening, is also rife with emotional nuances. As we venture forward, be prepared to dive even deeper, confronting the very emotions and wounds that come with being labeled the scapegoat. Yet, with every chapter, every page, and every word, remember: there is hope, strength, and a way out of the shadows. Your journey from scapegoat to summit is just beginning.

2

THE EMOTIONAL TOLL OF THE SCAPEGOAT
THE HIDDEN PAIN REVEALED

I remember a solitary walk I once took through a dense forest. The path, overgrown and seldom trodden, seemed to mirror my inner emotional journey. With every step, branches reached out, as if to remind me of the countless fingers that had pointed in blame, the numerous voices that whispered cruel judgments. Like many who bear the heavy mantle of the scapegoat, the forest of my emotions was thick with thorns of guilt, shame, and unworthiness.

Each one of us has an emotional tapestry, woven with the threads of our experiences, memories, and interactions. For those cast into the role of the family scapegoat, this fabric often bears the weight of dark shades—colors that represent years of undeserved blame, neglect, and isolation. This chapter is a voyage into that dense, sometimes daunting forest of emotions. It is essential, even painful, but undeniably necessary. Only by truly understanding and validating the emotional scars that mark a scapegoat's psyche can we begin the journey to healing.

For those who have felt the sting of being the 'designated problem,' I see you. I've been there. And for those who are yet to fathom the depth of such emotional turbulence, I invite you to step into this world, even if only for a while. It's time we shed light on the profound emotional consequences of being a scapegoat, to understand, to empathize, and ultimately, to pave the path to healing.

Imagine being the canvas upon which every mishap, every fault, and every discontent is painted. Over time, this constant barrage of blame and criticism begins to etch itself deeply, not just on the surface, but seeping into the very fibers of one's being. This is the daily reality for the scapegoat.

From forgotten chores to larger familial disputes, the scapegoat often finds themselves at the epicenter of blame. Even when logic might dictate otherwise, emotional dynamics warp perceptions, making the scapegoat the convenient target. It's a strange paradox, really. On one hand, the scapegoat becomes the most "visible" when things go wrong, but on the other, their true essence, their achievements, dreams, and genuine emotions often go unnoticed or undervalued.

With each unjust accusation, the voice inside begins to whisper: "Perhaps it truly is my fault." "Maybe I am the problem." "Do I really matter to them?" Slowly but surely, these external criticisms start to take root internally, leading the scapegoat to genuinely question their worth. It's not just about their place in the family anymore; it transcends that. They start doubting their value in friendships, in romantic relationships, and even in broader societal contexts.

Imagine constantly viewing yourself through a smudged lens, one that distorts and diminishes your true image.

That's the lens of unworthiness, and it's a tragically common accessory for many scapegoats. The pain isn't just in the criticisms received; it's in the love, recognition, and validation that's perpetually withheld.

Have you ever had a dream where you're accused of a crime you didn't commit, only to wake up with an unsettling knot in your stomach, the remnants of anxiety lingering? Now, imagine feeling that way, not in a fleeting dream, but in the very real moments of your waking life. This is the often suffocating cloak of guilt and shame that many scapegoats are draped in.

Guilt typically arises from a sense of having done something wrong. But what happens when this guilt is based on acts you didn't commit, or problems you didn't create? It becomes a phantom guilt - ever-present and haunting, even if baseless. The family scapegoat is familiar with this phantom. They're frequently the designated receptacle for the blame of others, leading them to feel responsible for the dysfunctions, failures, or misfortunes of the family, regardless of their actual involvement.

Closely related, yet even more insidious, is the feeling of shame. While guilt says, "I did something bad," shame whispers, "I am bad." It's a distinction with a vast difference. Being persistently accused and criticized, scapegoats often internalize this negativity, coming to view themselves as inherently flawed or defective. It's not merely about actions anymore; it's about their very identity.

The irony here is palpable. These feelings of guilt and shame are often misplaced. The scapegoat might be the most responsible person in the room, the most caring sibling, or the most diligent child. Yet, they're burdened with blame that belongs elsewhere. This emotional misdirection is not just an error in judgment but a profound act of injustice.

The impact of such relentless guilt and shame is profound. It shapes the way scapegoats interact with the world, often making them overly apologetic, hesitant to voice opinions, or fearful of judgment. They might constantly seek approval, validation, or even go to great lengths to avoid any situation where they might be blamed or criticized again.

In the theater of family dynamics, guilt and shame become the chains that bind the scapegoat, often keeping them anchored to a role that they neither chose nor deserve.

Navigating the labyrinth of guilt and shame is challenging, yet when we add the weight of loneliness to it, the journey becomes even more complex. The scapegoat, burdened by feelings they don't deserve, also grapples with the stark isolation that stems from their designated role. While guilt anchors them to past accusations and transgressions, real or imagined, loneliness propels them into an abyss of longing, seeking the warmth of genuine connection. It's a poignant twist: while the guilt keeps them tethered to their family, the ensuing loneliness makes them feel worlds apart. Let's delve deeper into this paradox of being surrounded yet feeling profoundly alone.

We often think of loneliness as a state reserved for those who are physically alone, but the heaviest form of loneliness can be felt when surrounded by people, especially loved ones. For the family scapegoat, loneliness is a haunting paradox. How can one feel so alone when they are constantly at the center of attention – albeit for the wrong reasons?

The scapegoat role, by its nature, is an isolating one. As the family's "designated problem," the scapegoat is emotionally separated from the rest. They're the black sheep, the odd one out, the one who doesn't quite "fit" with the rest. This role acts as an emotional exile, often causing the scapegoat to withdraw, expecting rejection or preparing for the next round of blame.

But the isolation isn't just emotional. At times, it's also physical. The scapegoat might be excluded from family events, left out of conversations, or even shunned to a degree. It's as if there's an invisible barrier around them, one that others are hesitant to cross. The message is clear: "You're different, and you don't belong."

This loneliness is deepened by the internal strife the scapegoat feels. They often grapple with a burning question: "If my own family, the people meant to love and protect me, treat me this way, what does it say about my place in the world?" Such thoughts amplify the feelings of isolation, extending them beyond family walls to broader social contexts.

Amid this isolation, there's a yearning. A yearning for genuine connection, understanding, and to be seen for who they truly are, not the distorted image painted by the scapegoating. They crave moments of belonging, where they're not on the defense, where they can let their guard down and just be.

The irony is that the scapegoat often develops a keen sense of empathy from their experiences. They're attuned to the emotions and needs of others, often because they know first-hand the pain of being misunderstood and isolated. And yet, this empathy, which could be a bridge to deep connections, often remains underutilized because of the walls they've built to protect themselves.

In essence, the scapegoat's journey is a paradoxical dance between seeking connection and fearing rejection. It's a silent cry to be understood, even when surrounded by the very voices that should be echoing understanding and love back to them.

Picture this: You're in a room where every sudden noise makes you jump. Every whisper sounds like a potential critic. Every side glance seems as if it might be directed at you, dissecting your every move. Welcome to the world of hyper-vigilance, an exhausting reality for many who bear the scapegoat label.

Hyper-vigilance is the body's high-alert system. For someone cast as the family's scapegoat, this system can be perpetually switched on. It's a protective mechanism, sharpened over years of bearing the brunt of blame, criticism, and disapproval. If you've always been the 'problem' or the 'reason' things go wrong, it makes perfect sense to develop an acute sensitivity to any signs of impending conflict or criticism. It's a survival tool, allowing the individual to anticipate and brace themselves for the next wave of blame or emotional upheaval.

However, this heightened state of alertness comes at a cost: anxiety. When one is continually bracing for impact, the body's stress response is always activated. Palpitations, sweaty palms, shallow breathing, and that gnawing feeling in the pit of the stomach become all too familiar companions. Anxiety is not just about fearing what might happen; it's also about living with the residue of what has repeatedly happened in the past.

Moreover, it's a bitter irony that the scapegoat, in their bid to avoid conflict or criticism, might inadvertently become more prone to it. Their nervous demeanor or over-compensatory behaviors can sometimes draw more attention and misunderstanding from family members, further entrenching them in the scapegoat role.

For the scapegoat, this cycle of hyper-vigilance leading to anxiety can be debilitating. But recognizing it, understanding its origins, and addressing its triggers is the first step towards breaking free and reclaiming mental and emotional equilibrium.

Navigating this emotional labyrinth, while each twist and turn further distorts our reflection, makes it paramount to understand the other ramifications of this role. As we pull back the curtains to expose these layers, it becomes evident that the consequences of being the family scapegoat reverberate beyond just our sense of worth. The very way we relate to others and how we perceive the world around us undergoes a transformation. Let's delve into one such impactful transformation: trust.

Ah, self-esteem – that inner sense of worth that guides our interactions with the world and dictates how high we allow ourselves to fly. For those donning the heavy cloak of the family scapegoat, the foundations of self-esteem are often shaky at best.

Years of bearing the role of the family scapegoat erode the bedrock of self-worth. When you are persistently reminded of your perceived inadequacies and failures, or consistently held responsible for the family's tribulations, it becomes almost second nature to doubt your value. You begin to question your worth not just within the family structure, but in the broader canvas of society. "If my own family sees me this way," you might think, "then surely, it must be true."

Over time, this chronic underestimation seeps into everyday actions. A reluctance to voice opinions fearing they might be 'wrong' yet again, hesitating to pursue opportunities because of an ingrained belief that you don't quite measure up, or even downplaying your achievements, attributing them to luck rather than competence.

But here's the stark reality: this distorted mirror the scapegoat is made to look into doesn't reflect their true worth. It's clouded by the unresolved traumas, insecurities, and dysfunctions of the family system. The scapegoat's eroded self-worth is a testament to the heavy burden they've shouldered, not an accurate measure of their inherent value.

Family is supposed to be our sanctuary—a refuge from the storms of the world. For many, it's the primary unit of unconditional love, trust, and support. But what happens when that trust is continuously broken? When the very foundation of faith you've constructed your self-worth upon is routinely chipped away by those who should be its staunchest guardians?

For the family scapegoat, the recurrent betrayals are not merely occasional disappointments; they are systematic demolitions of trust. Each unfair accusation, each unmerited blame, and every cold shoulder solidifies the belief: "If I can't trust my family, who can I trust?"

This erosion of trust within the family dynamics inadvertently spills into the scapegoat's relationships outside the family unit. Suspicion takes root. If the ones bound by blood could inflict such pain, would not a friend or a partner possibly do the same or even worse? Fear of betrayal becomes a near-constant companion, leading to a hesitancy in forming deep, meaningful connections. Every disagreement might be seen as a potential betrayal, every oversight as a sign of impending abandonment.

This isn't merely about being cautious; it's a profound fear of vulnerability. Why open yourself up to potential hurt when history has taught you that those who should love you unconditionally can wield such pain? The walls go up, not as a mark of strength, but as a defensive mechanism against further heartache.

Such challenges can make romantic relationships particularly tumultuous. The desire for connection battles with the impulse to protect oneself. Small misunderstandings can escalate quickly, driven by the ghost of past betrayals. Trust, once broken within the confines of the family, takes an immense effort to rebuild in the outside world.

Yet, it's crucial to recognize this pattern, for understanding is the first step towards healing. Only by acknowledging these trust issues can one begin the journey of restoring faith not just in others, but, more importantly, in oneself.

When we discuss the mental health implications of being scapegoated, it's essential to recognize that the emotional injuries inflicted aren't mere bruises that fade with time; they are deep wounds that, if left untreated, can fester and influence an individual's mental well-being profoundly.

Depression: One of the most immediate and enduring consequences of chronic scapegoating is depression. Feeling perpetually belittled, accused, and isolated can give rise to feelings of hopelessness and sadness. The constant message that "something is wrong with you" can anchor a person in a perpetual state of despondency, believing that they are inherently flawed, unlovable, or doomed to a life of unhappiness.

Anxiety Disorders: Stemming from the perpetual hyper-vigilance, anxiety becomes a daily companion for many scapegoats. The consistent state of alertness to potential criticisms or conflicts results in Generalized Anxiety Disorder (GAD) for some. This chronic anxiety isn't merely about specific family events but extends to an overarching sense of dread and worry about the future and one's place in the world.

Post-Traumatic Stress Disorder (PTSD): While commonly associated with war veterans, PTSD is a condition that can arise from various traumatic situations, including prolonged emotional abuse. For the scapegoat, repeated incidents of being unfairly blamed, shamed, or emotionally attacked can lead to this disorder. Flashbacks of painful events, nightmares, severe anxiety, and even uncontrollable thoughts about the events are hallmarks of PTSD.

Complex Post-Traumatic Stress Disorder (C-PTSD): An extension of PTSD, C-PTSD results from enduring complex trauma over a prolonged period, such as continuous emotional abuse in a family setting. Unlike PTSD, which can result from a single traumatic incident, C-PTSD arises from ongoing mistreatment. Scapegoats may experience feelings of powerlessness, disconnection from others, and a sense of being "different" or "damaged."

It's heartbreaking to think that the family—a unit meant for love, support, and protection—can be the root of such debilitating mental health challenges for the scapegoat. However, acknowledging these potential risks is paramount. By shining a light on these dark recesses of the scapegoat experience, there is hope for recognition, intervention, and ultimately, healing.

Not all scars are visible. The emotional and psychological trauma of being scapegoated doesn't just linger in the mind; it often translates into tangible behaviors. These behaviors, though sometimes discreet, can be a desperate cry for relief or a means of coping with the overpowering stress and pain that comes from being continuously marginalized and blamed.

Substance Abuse: One of the most common avenues of escape is through substance abuse. Alcohol, drugs, and other addictive substances offer a temporary reprieve, a fleeting moment where the pain subsides and the world becomes bearable. But this is a double-edged sword. While initially providing a semblance of relief, reliance on substances can lead to addiction, further complicating the scapegoat's life. Not only does this form of escapism fail to address the root of the pain, but it also introduces a myriad of additional problems, including health complications, financial strain, and potential legal troubles.

Self-Harm: A particularly harrowing response to the stress of being scapegoated is self-harm. For some, inflicting pain on oneself becomes a way to regain control, especially when their emotional world seems chaotic and uncontrollable. It's a physical manifestation of internal anguish, and for a fleeting moment, it can make the emotional pain recede. However, like substance abuse, this is a perilous path that only compounds the individual's struggles.

Other Forms of Escapism: Some scapegoats seek refuge in the virtual world, immersing themselves in video games, online communities, or endless hours of movies and TV shows. Others might dive deep into work, becoming workaholics, not out of passion but as a diversion from their emotional pain. Overeating, compulsive shopping, or engaging in risky behaviors can also be ways that scapegoats attempt to distract themselves from their emotional wounds.

While these behaviors might offer a temporary respite, they rarely provide lasting relief. Instead, they can become additional shackles, further imprisoning the scapegoat in a cycle of pain and escape. Recognizing these behaviors as consequences of the scapegoat role is crucial, for it is only through understanding the root cause that effective interventions and genuine healing can commence.

From the earliest days of my memory, there was an ever-present cloud, a vague sense that I was different from my siblings. While they bathed in the glow of our parents' attention, I often found myself in the shadows, wrestling with a confusing blend of longing and resentment.

Mornings were the hardest. I'd wake up to the sound of laughter from the next room, where my siblings would be animatedly discussing their dreams or planning the day's play. I, on the other hand, would often be tasked with chores or blamed for the slightest disarray, even if I wasn't its architect.

Family photos told a similar tale. While albums were filled with candid moments of my siblings - playing, laughing, or being embraced by our parents - my presence was more elusive. Most often, I'd be on the periphery, my smile not quite reaching my eyes, my posture slightly stooped, as if trying to occupy as little space as possible.

Birthdays, meant to be joyous occasions, often underlined my incongruity in the family tapestry. My siblings' celebrations would be grand affairs with friends, cakes, and countless presents. My own birthdays, however, were subdued, sometimes marked only by a hastily bought gift or, worse, forgotten altogether.

But perhaps what pained me most wasn't the overt neglect but the subtle, daily reminders of my lesser status: the interrupted stories, the constant comparisons, the sarcastic comments, and the unmet eyes. The message was clear, even if never explicitly articulated: I was the 'other', the invisible one.

Growing up, I often felt like a puzzle piece forced into the wrong jigsaw. It was in my early teenage years, when friendships deepened and I began sharing stories of family dynamics, that the contrast became impossible to ignore. Conversations with friends about their families were filled with tales of support and understanding, while my narratives were tainted with exclusion and blame.

One particular afternoon, as rain poured outside, I found myself in my best friend Clara's room, sharing tales of our recent family holidays. Clara spoke of shared laughter, games, and bonding while I recounted another story of being sidelined. As I narrated my experiences, a profound silence settled between us. Clara, with tears in her eyes, gently said, "It sounds like they always make you the scapegoat." That word - 'scapegoat' - it rang in my ears. I had never considered it before, but its weight was immediately recognizable.

The realization was both liberating and crushing. On one hand, there was relief in knowing that there was a term for my experience, that I wasn't alone, and that I wasn't imagining the imbalance. On the other, there was an overwhelming grief for all those years lost to unwarranted guilt and pain.

In school, while discussing a book where a character was continually unjustly blamed, a teacher commented on how families often assign roles unconsciously. That evening, I delved into articles and books, trying to understand the role of the scapegoat. With every line I read, my life seemed to unfurl before me – the patterns, the behaviors, the implications. It was as if a fog had lifted, revealing the harsh terrain I had been navigating all these years.

However, with clarity came anger, sadness, and a profound sense of betrayal. Why was I chosen for this role? What had I done to deserve this? The questions haunted my nights, leading to countless sleepless hours, staring at the ceiling, grappling with a torrent of emotions.

As the realization dawned upon me, I began to reflect on the myriad ways I had tried to navigate the turbulent waters of my family's dynamics. Over the years, my survival instincts had crafted an array of coping mechanisms, some of which offered temporary solace, while others further entangled me in the web of emotional pain.

1. Pleasing: One of my earliest and most persistent strategies was the pursuit of perfection. I believed that if I could be the perfect child - excelling in school, avoiding conflicts, and fulfilling every family obligation - the blaming would cease. But, of course, the goalposts kept shifting.

Each achievement was met with fleeting praise, quickly overshadowed by the next perceived shortcoming.

2. Withdrawal: As the years went by, and the weight of the scapegoat role grew heavier, I often sought refuge in isolation. My room became my sanctuary, a place where I could escape the accusations and judgments, even if just for a while. Books, music, and my own daydreams became portals to other worlds where I felt understood and valued.

3. Denial: At times, denial was the easiest path. I convinced myself that every family had its issues and that my experiences were just the typical family dynamics everyone talked about. By downplaying my emotions, I attempted to fit into a narrative that was more palatable, even if it was far from my reality.

4. Substance Use: As adolescence gave way to young adulthood, the allure of temporary escapes grew stronger. Alcohol and occasional drug use provided momentary relief from the relentless weight of my role. But with every morning after, the pain returned, often intensified by the guilt and shame of my actions.

5. Seeking External Validation: Starved for appreciation within the familial walls, I began to seek validation outside. Friendships, romantic relationships, and even casual acquaintances became platforms where I desperately sought affirmation. While some of these bonds were genuine, others were mere reflections of my own insecurities, further complicating my emotional landscape.

6. Therapy and Self-help: Eventually, the weight of my emotions became too much to bear alone. Seeking professional help, I began attending therapy sessions.

Through these meetings, I unearthed deeply buried traumas and started the process of healing. Reading self-help books and attending support groups also became instrumental in understanding my role and seeking ways to break free.

The journey was, and continues to be, a mosaic of highs and lows, of successes and setbacks. While some coping mechanisms served as lifelines, others threatened to pull me further into the abyss. Recognizing, understanding, and actively working on them was the first step towards reclaiming my narrative and self-worth.

As the tapestry of my life began to unravel thread by thread, amidst the shadows of past experiences, a resilient spark began to emerge. It wasn't a sudden epiphany but rather a gradual awareness. The very challenges that sought to break me also held the seeds of my redemption.

It began with small moments of clarity. A kind word from a stranger, a therapeutic breakthrough, or the simple act of standing up for myself became significant milestones. I slowly began to recognize that while I had been assigned the role of the scapegoat, I was not bound to it. My worth was not defined by others' perceptions but by the strength of character I had developed and the compassionate heart that still managed to beat inside me, despite the odds.

It was in these moments that I understood the essence of resilience. Resilience wasn't about bypassing pain or denying its existence. It was about embracing it, learning from it, and using it as a catalyst for growth. Each scar I bore became a testament to battles fought and survived, and with each victory, no matter how small, my desire for change grew stronger.

I yearned for a life where I was the author of my own narrative, where the chains of the past no longer held me captive. This yearning, this ember of hope, became the guiding light, leading me out of the darkness and into the journey of healing. And as we will discover in the subsequent chapters, this journey, while deeply personal, is also universal. For every scapegoat out there, know this: there is a path forward, one that leads to empowerment, self-acceptance, and ultimately, liberation.

In this chapter, we delved into the labyrinthine emotional terrain navigated by scapegoats. From the very outset, it's evident that the weight they bear is immense, their experiences echoing with feelings of unworthiness, guilt, shame, and a profound sense of isolation. These emotional states, exacerbated over time, can lead to severe psychological scars, which manifest in trust issues, mental health disorders, and self-destructive behaviors.

The personal story we explored served as a poignant testament to these struggles, shining a light on the lived realities of those relegated to this painful role. Yet, even amidst the darkness of their narratives, glimmers of resilience and hope can emerge. It's a powerful reminder that while the past shapes us, it doesn't define our entirety.

Recognizing the challenges faced by scapegoats isn't merely an exercise in empathy. It's a call to action. Acknowledging their pain, understanding its origins, and addressing its repercussions are vital steps in the healing process. As we journey deeper in the chapters to come, we will pivot towards this process of recognition, understanding, and healing. The story of the scapegoat is not just one of suffering, but also of transformation and redemption.

3

RECOGNIZING THE PATTERNS
SPOTTING THE INVISIBLE CHAINS

On a personal retreat some years ago, nestled among the pines and in the embrace of solitude, I remember reading a quote by Lao Tzu: "Knowing others is intelligence; knowing yourself is true wisdom." It struck a chord. So many of us, in our quest for validation, often overlook the importance of understanding our own narratives, especially when they've been written by someone else. The profound journey from being a scapegoat to self-liberation is as much about rewriting these narratives as it is about recognizing them in the first place.

I know this all too well. In my own life, I've felt the weight of unearned blame, the sting of misplaced anger, and the chilling isolation of being the family's emotional landfill. But it was during my doctoral years, surrounded by a maze of psychological theories and journals, that I truly began connecting the dots. And as I delved deeper into the world of family dynamics, the patterns became starkly evident. Not just in clinical cases or textbooks, but in the raw, real narratives of countless individuals who, like myself, had been cast as the 'scapegoat'.

Recognizing these patterns was like finding the first piece of a complex jigsaw puzzle. It didn't immediately solve the mystery, but it offered a starting point—a beacon of clarity in a fog of confusion. Self-awareness, as I've come to understand, is not merely a reflective exercise; it's a radical act of reclaiming power. It's about interrupting cycles of harm, drawing boundaries, and advocating for oneself.

So, why is recognizing patterns so pivotal? Because buried beneath these patterns lies the truth of your experiences. It's akin to finally understanding the language of a foreign land you've inadvertently found yourself in. And with that understanding, the power to navigate shifts from the hands of those around you to firmly within your grasp. You start seeing the red flags, not as isolated incidents, but as threads of a larger tapestry. And suddenly, the intricate dance of family dynamics, with its steps of blame, deflection, and denial, becomes transparent.

In this chapter, I invite you to embark on a journey of recognition. Together, we will unearth the signs, the subtle nudges, and the glaring indicators that you, dear reader, have been cast in the role of the family scapegoat. And as we do, remember that recognizing these patterns is not about assigning blame. Instead, it's about understanding, healing, and ultimately, transformation. For it's only when we truly see that we can begin to change.

So, pour yourself a warm cup of tea or find a cozy corner, and let's delve into the world of patterns and signs that have, for so long, been waiting for you to see them.

Growing up, did you ever play that game of 'hot potato'? The frantic tossing of a potato (or any small object, really) from one person to another, trying to avoid being the one holding it when the music stops? Now, imagine the potato being blame, and the game never truly ends. That's the life of a scapegoat in a nutshell.

It was my 12th birthday. The cake was on the table, candles lit, and as my family gathered around, a sudden crash echoed from the living room. A vase – a family heirloom – lay in shards. Before the dust could settle, or anyone even saw the cat responsible for the mishap sprinting away, eyes turned to me, accusatory fingers pointed. "What did you do, Emily?" My protests of innocence were drowned in the chorus of blame, and my birthday song was replaced with a lecture. An isolated incident, you might think. But for a scapegoat, this is the soundtrack to their life.

Being consistently and unfairly blamed is a trademark experience of the scapegoat. You become the family's go-to explanation for anything that goes wrong, irrespective of logic or actual events. It's like having an invisible bullseye painted on your back. The dog chewed up the newspaper? It's your fault for not watching it. The milk went sour? Surely, you did something. It can get so absurd that you'd be blamed for a rainstorm during a family picnic!

This chronic misplacement of blame is not merely about finding an easy outlet for frustrations. It's an insidious pattern that seeks to reinforce the idea that the scapegoat is inherently flawed or responsible. Over time, this consistent barrage of blame, especially for issues you have no control over, can lead to self-doubt. You begin to internalize the blame, constantly second-guessing yourself, and sometimes even apologizing for things you haven't done. After all, if everyone says it's your fault, they must be right... right?

The truth is, being perpetually blamed is less about your actions and more about the dysfunctional dynamics within the family unit. When accountability is avoided, it's easier to have a 'designated culprit' than to face underlying issues. But remember, every time you're blamed without reason, it's not a reflection of your worth or character. It's merely a symptom of a deeper familial ailment, one that you're neither responsible for nor required to cure.

As we journey ahead, dear reader, you might find resonance in these signs. Perhaps a memory might be triggered, or an old wound might throb. Hold onto that self-awareness, embrace it, but also be gentle with yourself. For in recognition, there's liberation waiting to be claimed.

Have you ever experienced the uncanny sensation of being a fish out of water? Not the literal, flopping-on-the-shore kind, but that sinking feeling of being profoundly out of place. Now, imagine this sensation not in a room full of strangers, but amidst the very people who share your genes and home - your family.

I remember a family photo from a few years back. There we all were, smiling, posed in front of our cozy little house. But even as my eyes traced familiar faces, an uneasy feeling settled in my heart. It was as if I were looking at a picture of someone else's family, with me inexplicably photo-bombing their moment. My clothes, my posture, even my smile – everything seemed slightly off, as though I was a puzzle piece from another set, desperately trying to fit in.

This feeling of "otherness" is a gnawing constant for many scapegoats. It's an emotional exile, an invisible barrier that separates you from familial camaraderie. While others share inside jokes, reminisce shared memories, or indulge in collective activities, the scapegoat often feels like an observer, an outsider. As the family gathers around the TV or dinner table, you might find a corner, mentally and some-times physically distanced, wondering why you don't quite gel.

The irony is heartbreaking. Home is supposed to be our haven, the place where we are loved unconditionally, where we belong without pretense. But for the scapegoat, home often morphs into a theater of alienation. Family events, holidays, or reunions that should spell joy and connection instead become arenas of isolation.

Yet, here's a nugget of wisdom I've gleaned: It's not *you* that's out of place; it's the distorted family dynamic that places you there. The gap you feel isn't a lack within you but a manifestation of the role unfairly thrust upon you. It's like being cast as the villain in a play without ever audi-tioning for the part. The script might label you the 'odd one out', but off-stage, in the grand drama of life, you have every right to belong, to connect, to be embraced for who you truly are.

To the reader silently nodding, recognizing this feeling all too well: Your worth is not determined by how seamlessly you fit into someone else's picture or narrative. Authentic belonging is not about changing yourself to fit in, but finding spaces where your authentic self is cherished and celebrated.

Do you remember the childhood game of "tug-of-war"? Two teams, pulling on either end of a rope, trying their hardest not to be pulled over a marker or, in some cases, into a muddy pit? Now, imagine playing that game every day, with no respite, and often without allies on your side. This, dear reader, is a glimpse into the emotional weariness that accompanies the life of a scapegoat.

One sunny afternoon, my niece asked me to play with her. The game? Defending a sandcastle against waves. As wave after wave crashed, we tirelessly rebuilt, fortifying our defenses, only to see our efforts crumble again. The sun set, and with tired arms and defeated spirits, we watched the tide wash our fortress away. It struck me how this mirrored the life I had been leading, always defending, always rebuilding, and often feeling swept away.

The psyche of a scapegoat is perennially in a defensive stance. Whether it's deflecting blame, justifying actions, or constantly trying to prove one's worth, it's like being a gladiator in an arena where battles never cease. Each day, you don your armor, knowing that misunderstandings, blame, and confrontations await.

This relentless need to defend oneself, to correct miscon-strued narratives, or to achieve to gain even an iota of approval drains energy at a profound level. It's more than just physical tiredness; it's an emotional and mental fatigue that seeps into the very core, sometimes making even the simplest tasks feel like Herculean challenges. It's waking up tired and going to bed even more so.

In the journey of the scapegoat, proving oneself isn't just about showcasing abilities or talents. It's about proving one's basic worthiness, humanity, and the right to be treated with dignity and respect. When these foundational aspects of self are constantly called into question, the resultant exhaustion is immeasurable.

But I want you to remember something: you're not alone in this. Across the pages of this book, I extend a hand, not just as an author but as a fellow traveler on this tumultuous path. And with every word, I hope to help lighten that emotional load, even if just a bit.

As we move forward, keep this mantra close to heart:

> I am enough, not because I prove it, but because I exist.

On to our next sign.

Stories are powerful. They shape cultures, move hearts, and cement legacies. But, in the household of the scapegoat, they often play a less romantic role. They become tools of confinement, sketching distorted pictures and holding captive in frames of falsehood.

When I was 15, during a family gathering, an aunt recounted a tale from my childhood. Apparently, at the tender age of four, I had caused quite the scene by "stealing" cookies and blaming it on our pet cat. The room erupted in laughter, and I sat there, cheeks burning, wishing I could melt into the ground. Here's the thing: I never took those cookies. But this story had been repeated so often, painted with such vivid brushes of mischief and deceit, that it became a family legend, an undeniable testament to my "devious nature." And it wasn't just about cookies. There were countless other tales, each crafting an image of me that suited the narrative of the family's designated troublemaker.

Family narratives surrounding the scapegoat often follow a fixed script: painting them as the instigator, the problem child, the black sheep. Whether it's childhood pranks blown out of proportion, genuine mistakes eternally spotlighted, or even accomplishments twisted into tales of deception or mere luck, the scapegoat's story is relentlessly edited to fit a pre-decided mold. The most frustrating part? Many times, these narratives emerge independent of actual events, shaped more by perceptions and biases than reality.

These stories can sting, but they also serve a larger purpose for the family unit. They reinforce roles, ensure the scapegoat remains confined in their assigned position, and provide others a comfortable lens through which they can view, and judge, the scapegoat's every action. And often, these narratives are so consistently and convincingly relayed that even outsiders, with no first-hand knowledge of events, buy into them.

But here's a silver lining: just as stories have the power to bind, they also hold the potential to set free. Recognizing the patterns in these family tales, understanding their origins and motives, can be the first step in reclaiming your narrative. It's time to pick up the pen, rewrite those chapters, and craft a story that truly reflects who you are, not who they want you to be.

Remember this: stories evolve, and so do we. Our next exploration dives deeper into the complex web of family roles. Buckle up; it's going to be a revealing ride.

Every family is a unique tapestry of relationships, roles, and dynamics. And within this intricate weave, there often emerge two figures standing in stark contrast to each other: the Golden Child and the Scapegoat. I've lived this tale firsthand, with my younger brother, Ben, shining brilliantly as the golden boy, while I, seemingly by default, was cast in the shadows.

The Golden Child, as the title suggests, can do no wrong. Their achievements, however minor, are celebrated with grandeur. Their mistakes, on the rare occasions they're acknowledged, are swiftly brushed under the proverbial rug. They are painted in colors of success, virtue, and perfection, often serving as the benchmark against which others are measured. In our family, Ben's B-grade was applauded, while my A was met with, "Why not an A+?" And if Ben did err, somehow, it circled back to being my fault.

In stark contrast stands the Scapegoat. If the Golden Child is the sun, the scapegoat is the stormy cloud. Their achievements are downplayed, their efforts often over-looked or, worse, ridiculed. Mistakes? They're not just acknowledged but amplified, becoming the stuff of family legends (recall the cookie saga?). They are the ones who bear the brunt, absorbing the family's collective frustrations, failures, and disappointments. It's no surprise then that family gatherings often felt like tiptoeing through a minefield, with every step being compared to Ben's graceful strides.

The dynamics this creates are palpable. There's a tangible tension, an unsaid rivalry that neither the Golden Child nor the Scapegoat may have asked for. Jealousy, resentment, guilt, and a slew of mixed emotions churn beneath the surface. Birthdays, holidays, and family events, which should be occasions of joy, can turn into battlegrounds of validation and attention. The worst part? This divide often spills over, affecting relationships with extended family, friends, and even into adulthood.

It's worth noting, however, that neither role - Golden Child nor Scapegoat - is particularly enviable. While it might seem that the Golden Child has it easy, they too are confined, albeit in a golden cage. The pressure to perpetually perform, to maintain that facade of perfection, can be overwhelming. Ben once confessed, during a rare vulnerable moment, how suffocating the weight of expectations felt.

So, the next time you find yourself envying the Golden Child in your family or feeling the sting of being the Scapegoat, remember: both are roles assigned, not identities chosen. And roles, with awareness and effort, can be redefined.

While the Golden Child and the Scapegoat stand at two extremes, there are other characters in this familial play, some who enable this dynamic and others who watch in silence. Let's turn the spotlight on them, shall we?

In the theater of family dynamics, the Enabler may not stand center stage, but their influence is unmistakably pervasive, shaping the plot in profound ways. They function as the catalyst, fueling the scapegoating narrative, sometimes overtly and at other times in nuanced, covert ways. Understanding the role of the Enabler is crucial to demystifying the scapegoat phenomenon.

So, who is the Enabler? On the surface, they might appear as the peacekeeper, the mediator, or even the voice of reason. However, upon closer inspection, their actions (or lack thereof) perpetuate the established family roles. They might dismiss the scapegoat's feelings, downplaying the impact of the family's behavior with statements like "It's just the way things are" or "They didn't mean it that way." By doing so, they inadvertently (or sometimes intentionally) validate the unequal treatment.

A classic portrayal of the Enabler is the parent who soothes the scapegoat after a bout of unjust blame, not by addressing the injustice but by offering platitudes like "You're stronger, you can handle it" or "Don't let it get to you." While their intentions might be rooted in comfort, the underlying message is clear: the status quo is acceptable, and the scapegoat should bear it gracefully.

Active enablers are more direct in their support of the scapegoating dynamic. They might jump onto the blame bandwagon, adding their own accusations or criticisms. They reinforce the narrative by amplifying the negative stories about the scapegoat or dismissing their achievements. In my family, Aunt Clara was a prime example. She'd embellish stories of my "misdemeanors," painting them in shades darker than they were, further cementing my role.

However, passive enablers are more subtle and, arguably, more insidious. They may not participate in the scapegoating directly, but their silence speaks volumes. They witness the unfair treatment, the hurtful comments, the blatant favoritism, and yet choose not to intervene. Their inaction, whether rooted in fear, indifference, or a misguided sense of not wanting to 'rock the boat,' further entrenches the scapegoat's role, as it sends a tacit message of agreement.

The role of the Enabler, be it active or passive, is multifaceted. Some may genuinely believe they're doing what's best for the family, preserving harmony by not challenging the established dynamics. Others might be motivated by self-preservation, avoiding the spotlight or potential backlash. And then there are those who, consciously or unconsciously, derive a sense of power or superiority from the dynamic.

Recognizing and understanding the Enabler's role is an essential step in challenging the scapegoating narrative. Only by addressing the root enablers can one hope to rewrite the family script.

While the Enabler plays a pivotal part, there are bystanders in this narrative who, though silent, have a tale of their own to tell.

In the intricate web of family dynamics, the Silent Observers are often the most enigmatic characters. Distinct from the Enablers, who actively or passively contribute to the scapegoating, these individuals recognize the unfairness, discern the dysfunctional patterns, and yet, for various reasons, remain in the shadows, their voices muted. Their silence, whether intentional or unintentional, has profound implications for the scapegoat, subtly reinforcing the prevailing dynamics.

For the scapegoat, the silence of these Observers can be particularly painful. There's an inherent trust that those who see injustice will speak out against it. When that expectation is unmet, feelings of isolation and betrayal intensify. The scapegoat may wonder, "If even those who see the unfairness won't stand with me, then perhaps I truly am at fault."

So, why do these Silent Observers choose not to intervene? The reasons are multifarious:

1. Fear of Retaliation: One of the most common reasons for silence is the fear of backlash. The Observer might worry that by standing up for the scapegoat, they might become the next target. This fear, while seemingly self-serving, is often rooted in personal experiences or observations of how dissenting voices are treated within the family.

2. Desire for Harmony: Some Observers value family harmony above all else. They believe that confronting the issue might create more discord, so they opt for a silent compromise, hoping that the storm will pass without their involvement.

3. Uncertainty on How to Intervene: Recognizing a problem and knowing how to address it are two distinct things. Some Observers might be aware of the scapegoating but feel ill-equipped to challenge it or fear that their intervention might exacerbate the situation.

4. Conformity to Family Norms: In families with deeply ingrained traditions and norms, there's immense pressure to conform. Observers might disagree with the scapegoating privately but choose not to express their dissent openly, fearing ostracization or ridicule.

5. Belief in Passive Support: Some Observers may think that by providing quiet, behind-the-scenes support to the scapegoat, they're doing enough. They might offer a listening ear or occasional words of comfort, believing these gestures are sufficient.

While the Silent Observers' reasons for staying muted may vary, the impact of their silence on the scapegoat remains consistent. It reinforces the legitimacy of the scapegoat's role, amplifying feelings of loneliness and validation of the family's narrative.

For change to occur, it's crucial for the Silent Observers to recognize the weight of their inaction. Their choice to speak up or continue withholding can significantly shape the family's dynamics. Breaking the cycle of scapegoating often begins when these Observers find their voice, standing in solidarity with the scapegoat, and challenging the established narrative.

As we delve deeper into family interactions, it becomes evident that external influences too play a pivotal role in shaping these dynamics.

Across various civilizations and epochs, the dynamics within the family microcosm often mirror the larger societal and cultural constructs. One cannot overlook the influence of societal norms and cultural traditions when dissecting the scapegoat phenomenon within families. At times, these norms validate the treatment of the scapegoat, while at other moments, they challenge and reshape familial dynamics.

Scapegoating isn't solely a family affair; it has been embedded in larger societal structures for millennia. Historical instances of scapegoating can be seen as reflections of an inherent human tendency to offload blame onto an 'other', be it an individual, a group, or even an entire community.

1. Ancient Rituals: In many ancient civilizations, a literal scapegoat — often an actual goat — was symbolically burdened with the sins of the community and then driven into the wilderness, effectively carrying away the community's wrongdoings. This ritual, found in ancient Judaic practices, highlights a deep-seated human need to cleanse the collective conscience by placing blame on a singular entity.

2. Witch Hunts: The infamous European witch hunts between the 15th and 18th centuries offer a chilling example of societal scapegoating. Women, especially those who were outsiders or defied societal norms, were blamed for societal ills, leading to mass hysteria, trials, and executions.

3. Racial and Ethnic Scapegoating: Throughout history, minority groups, be it based on race, religion, or ethnicity, have often been made scapegoats, blamed for economic downturns, diseases, or political unrest. Examples include the persecution of Jews in various European countries, the internment of Japanese-Americans during World War II, and the discrimination against various ethnic groups during times of societal strain.

Such large-scale societal scapegoating offers a macro perspective on the dynamics we observe within families. When cultural norms legitimize the casting out or blaming of a particular member or group, families that internalize these values might replicate similar behaviors on a smaller scale.

However, society and culture are not static; they evolve. Modern-day movements championing inclusivity, mental health awareness, and challenging traditional power dynamics are reshaping how families perceive and treat their members. These progressive shifts challenge the entrenched scapegoating patterns, offering hope for those trapped in such roles.

In essence, while history is replete with examples where societal and cultural norms have endorsed scapegoating, the tides are turning. As society becomes more introspective and values individual rights and well-being, families are prompted to question and, ideally, rectify age-old dysfunctional patterns.

Yet, while societal norms play a crucial role, so do immediate influences such as peers and the omnipresent force of social media.

The interpersonal dynamics within a family don't exist in isolation; they're in constant interaction with the outer world. One potent source of this external influence is our peer group: friends, colleagues, neighbors, and acquaintances. They play a pivotal role in either reinforcing or challenging the scapegoat narrative within the family.

At times, friends or acquaintances might unintentionally, or even deliberately, echo the negative perceptions held by the family about the scapegoat. This can occur due to several reasons:

1. Shared Cultural or Societal Beliefs: Peers, especially those from the same cultural or societal background, might share the same biases or prejudices as the family. For instance, in cultures where academic excellence is highly prized, a child who doesn't conform to these expectations might be viewed as 'less than' not only by their family but also by the wider community.

2. Misinformation: Often, narratives spun within families find their way outside. If the scapegoat's role is characterized by false stories or exaggerated claims, friends or acquaintances who hear these narratives might believe them without seeking the scapegoat's perspective.

3. Conformity: Peer groups have their dynamics, and the desire to fit in can lead individuals to adopt the majority's view without questioning. If a scapegoat is seen in a certain light by most, others might conform to this view to avoid conflict or out of a need to belong.

However, peers can also be a breath of fresh air, offering an external perspective that challenges the family's narrative:

1. Objective Observations: Friends who interact with the scapegoat outside the family setting might see them in a different light. They might recognize their talents, empathize with their struggles, and appreciate their unique qualities, countering the negative image painted by the family.

2. Shared Experiences: Acquaintances who've experienced similar family dynamics can offer validation and support. They can relate to the scapegoat's feelings, reassure them of their worth, and suggest coping strategies.

3. Open Conversations: Sometimes, a mere conversation can lead to an epiphany. By discussing their family situation with understanding peers, scapegoats might gain insights into the dynamics at play, realizing that the blame placed upon them isn't always warranted.

In conclusion, peers can either perpetuate the scapegoat's plight or act as a beacon of hope. Their influence underscores the importance of cultivating supportive, understanding, and open-minded relationships outside of one's family. After all, sometimes, it takes an outsider's perspective to see things clearly.

Up next, we delve into the digital realm to explore how social media impacts the scapegoat narrative.

In our hyper-connected world, social media has become an integral facet of many people's lives, acting as both a mirror reflecting societal attitudes and a platform amplifying personal narratives. For the scapegoat, social media can be a double-edged sword, serving to magnify their experiences, whether for better or for worse.

Amplification of Public Shaming:

1. Spotlight on Mistakes: One small error or misjudgment, when captured and shared, can go viral within hours. For the scapegoat, this is especially perilous as they are already positioned as the 'default' target. A mistake that might be overlooked or forgiven in another family member can become a focal point of ridicule when associated with the scapegoat.

2. Fueling Family Narratives: Negative portrayals or stories about the scapegoat can spread like wildfire on social platforms, further entrenching the established family narrative. This not only impacts the scapegoat's self-perception but also affects how outsiders perceive them.

3. Online Bullying and Harassment: The anonymity provided by the internet can embolden individuals to act more maliciously than they would in person. If the scapegoat is already facing issues offline, online platforms might provide yet another avenue for tormentors to continue their bullying.

Potential for Validation and Support:

1. Finding One's Tribe: Social media platforms allow scapegoats to connect with others who've had similar experiences. Support groups, forums, and online communities can provide a space for shared stories, mutual encouragement, and strategies for coping.

2. Raising Awareness: By sharing their stories, scapegoats can raise awareness about the adverse effects of such family dynamics. This not only educates others but can also challenge and change societal perceptions.

3. Affirmation and Positive Reinforcement: While social media can be a source of negativity, it can also be a platform for love and support. Comments, likes, and shares can act as affirmations, reminding the scapegoat that they are valued and understood.

4. Access to Resources: The internet is rife with information, self-help guides, therapeutic resources, and expert advice. A scapegoat seeking understanding or tools for personal growth can find a treasure trove of resources online.

In sum, the digital age's vast interconnected web can either entangle the scapegoat further in negative narratives or provide a lifeline leading them to a supportive community and self-affirmation. The key lies in how one navigates this landscape, armed with awareness and a critical mind, discerning the genuine support from the mere noise.

Navigating the labyrinth of family dynamics can be a challenging endeavor, especially when one finds oneself in the scapegoat role. The patterns that emerge – from the relentless blame game to the feeling of not truly belonging within one's own family – paint a picture that many may find tragically familiar. Emotional exhaustion, negative narratives, and the polarized treatment between the scapegoat and the golden child all compound the experience, making it a heavy burden to bear.

However, as with many challenges in life, recognition is the first step towards transformation. By being aware of these signs and understanding the role of various family members and external influences, an individual can start to rewrite their story. Societal norms, peer pressures, and the omnipresent influence of social media are essential facets to consider, for they shape perceptions, validate experiences, or, at times, exacerbate the scapegoat's ordeal.

The beauty of self-awareness lies in its power to pave the way for change. The sheer act of recognizing these patterns empowers the scapegoat to challenge established dynamics and forge a path towards healthier relationships, both within the family and outside of it.

As we conclude this chapter, dear reader, we urge you to take a moment for introspection. Reflect on your experiences and relationships. Do these patterns resonate with your personal narrative? Remember, knowledge equips you with the tools to instigate change. No longer must you remain a passive actor in your life story. By acknowledging and understanding these patterns, you hold the power to alter the narrative, championing a future filled with understanding, love, and acceptance.

In the coming chapters, we will delve deeper into strategies and methods to navigate, challenge, and ultimately break free from the scapegoat role. But for now, embrace the power of recognition and let it be the beacon that guides you towards healing and transformation.

4

BREAKING THE CYCLE
THE PATH TO LIBERATION

Each dawn brings with it the promise of a new day, a fresh opportunity to rise, reinvent, and reclaim. This isn't just poetic waxing; it's the essence of human resilience and the bedrock of personal transformation. As you turn this page, know that you're not just moving to another chapter of a book, but stepping onto a path of empowerment, where the shadows cast by the scapegoat label begin to recede.

Over the years, I've found solace in the words of the great Maya Angelou: "You may not control all the events that happen to you, but you can decide not to be reduced by them." These words encapsulate the spirit of our journey. The family dynamics that designated you the scapegoat were not of your making, but challenging and altering this narrative lies within your power. Remember, the world outside mirrors the beliefs held within. Recognizing your worth and understanding that you don't have to be confined to a role unjustly thrust upon you is pivotal to changing both your internal beliefs and external circumstances.

With every breath, remind yourself: transformation is not just possible; it's a promise you owe to your essence. This chapter, my dear reader, is about tapping into that indomitable spirit, breaking free, and soaring beyond the confines of past labels and limitations. Because every scapegoat has wings, and it's high time you found yours.

During one of my lowest moments, when the weight of the scapegoat label felt unbearably heavy, I stumbled upon a revelation in the stillness of the night. While lying in bed, drenched in moonlight and introspection, it dawned on me: the key to change was not outside of me but nestled deep within. Before I could alter the narrative others had crafted for me, I had to delve deep into the narratives I held about myself. This journey began with self-awareness and reflection.

Self-awareness is not just about understanding who you are; it's about deciphering who you've been told to be and distinguishing between the two. Let's dive into this transformative process:

1. Introspection: The first step is to dedicate moments of quiet introspection. It might seem simple, but in the hustle and bustle of life, we often neglect this crucial aspect. Carve out time to sit quietly, journal, or even meditate. Allow thoughts and emotions to surface without judgment.

2. Understanding Emotions: Being the family scapegoat can be a rollercoaster of emotions – from anger to sadness, resentment to hopelessness. Acknowledge each emotion, but more importantly, ask yourself why you feel a certain way. Is it because of an event that happened, a comment someone made, or a memory that resurfaced?

Understand that your feelings are valid, but also be conscious of how they shape your responses and interactions.

3. Identifying Triggers: With time and introspection, you'll begin to notice patterns—specific comments, actions, or situations that trigger negative emotions or reinforce the scapegoat label. For me, it was the subtle jabs at family dinners or the comparisons with siblings. Identifying these triggers is essential, not to brace yourself for hurt, but to equip yourself for change.

Throughout this process, I found solace in a quote from Carl Jung:

> Until you make the unconscious conscious, it will direct your life and you will call it fate.

Recognizing and understanding the subconscious scripts that were written for you, and sometimes by you, is the first significant step toward rewriting your story. In the upcoming sections, we'll delve into strategies to communicate, seek external insights, and empower your responses. But always remember, every journey of transformation begins with a single step inward.

It was during a particularly heated family dinner that I realized the enormous power of words, and more importantly, how they're delivered. I had been on the receiving end of a familiar line of criticism and felt a swell of emotions ready to erupt. But rather than launching into a defensive tirade, I chose a different approach. Instead of placing blame, I used "I" statements, conveying my feelings without hurling accusations. The difference in the response I received was like night and day. Here's how you can harness the power of effective communication in your interactions:

1. The Power of "I" Statements: Traditional blame phrases like "You always put me down!" can make the listener defensive, shutting down the lines of communication. On the contrary, "I" statements such as "I feel hurt when my efforts are dismissed" center the conversation around your feelings, rather than pointing fingers. This subtle shift can open doors to understanding and empathy.

2. Be Specific: Instead of using general terms, get specific. Instead of saying, "You never listen to me," you might say, "I felt unheard when I shared my news about work and the topic was quickly changed."

3. Stay Calm: Remember, emotions can be contagious. If you approach a conversation with a raised voice or aggressive tone, you can expect the other person to raise their defenses. Deep breaths, steady tones, and a calm demeanor can make your words resonate more effectively.

4. Practice Active Listening: Communication isn't just about speaking; it's equally about listening. When you give someone your full attention and truly listen to their perspective, you set an example of how you wish to be treated in return.

5. Seek Clarification: Sometimes, misunderstandings arise from misconceptions or misinterpretations. Before reacting, ask questions to ensure you've fully understood the other person's viewpoint. "When you said ____, did you mean ____?" can often clear up potential conflicts before they escalate.

6. Reiterate Your Love and Commitment: Especially when dealing with family, it's crucial to remind them that your desire to communicate better stems from a place of love. You're not attacking or accusing; you're seeking a more harmonious relationship.

Throughout my journey, I discovered that communication is a bridge. One side is anchored in your feelings and experiences, and the other in the possibility of understanding and mutual respect. And while it's not always easy, especially in deeply ingrained family dynamics, every genuine attempt at open communication is a step toward strengthening that bridge. In the next sections, we'll explore how seeking external perspectives can further bolster your journey of self-advocacy and empowerment.

In one of my lowest moments, when the weight of the scapegoat label felt like a boulder pressing on my chest, a close friend suggested I see a therapist. I remember laughing it off, thinking, "Why would I pay someone to listen to my family drama?" But in that desperate hour, I gave it a shot, and boy, was I in for an awakening!

1. An Objective Lens: Family dynamics are often mired in decades of history, making it challenging to view situations impartially. Therapists, counselors, or even trusted friends can offer a fresh, objective perspective. They aren't embroiled in the family drama, making them invaluable in pointing out patterns or behaviors you might have overlooked.

2. Safe Space to Vent: Let's face it, constantly discussing family issues with friends can strain relationships. A therapy session or support group provides a designated environment to freely express your feelings without fear of judgment or overburdening someone.

3. Validation: This was perhaps the most unexpected and cherished benefit for me. Hearing an external party validate my feelings and experiences had an incredibly healing effect. It's easy to doubt yourself when you've been pigeonholed into a particular role within the family, but external validation can serve as a balm to those self-inflicted wounds of doubt.

4. Skill Building: Professionals often equip you with coping mechanisms, communication techniques, and strategies to navigate challenging family interactions. These skills aren't just theoretical; they're tried, tested, and tailored to your unique situation.

5. Exploration of Deep-Seated Issues: Sometimes, the scapegoat label is just the tip of the iceberg. Therapists can help delve deep into underlying issues, childhood traumas, or unresolved conflicts that contribute to your current dynamics.

6. Finding Your Tribe: Support groups, especially those centered around family dynamics or specific issues, can be a godsend. Sharing experiences, hearing others' stories, and realizing you're not alone in your struggle can be incredibly empowering.

7. Accountability: Regularly attending therapy or support groups ensures a level of accountability. It's a scheduled check-in, a dedicated time to focus on your healing and growth.

In retrospect, seeking external viewpoints was like turning on a flashlight in a dark room. Suddenly, things that were tripping me up became visible. Patterns emerged. And with that clarity came the power to change, adapt, and heal. If you've been teetering on the fence about seeking external guidance, I urge you to give it a chance. The perspective you'll gain might just be the key to unlocking a healthier, happier you. Next, we'll delve into crafting empowering responses, turning the tables on scapegoating behavior with grace and strength.

One balmy summer evening, during a family barbecue, I overheard a snide comment directed at me from a distant aunt. "Emily's always been the odd one out, hasn't she?" she remarked with a smirk. As the laughter bubbled up around me, the familiar sting of humiliation crept up my cheeks. But instead of sinking into my usual seat of discomfort, I took a deep breath and responded, "Well, Aunt Linda, being the 'odd one' has taught me to be unique and resilient. I wouldn't have it any other way." The courtyard fell silent, but the strength I felt in that moment was deafening.

Addressing scapegoating behaviors with empowering responses doesn't mean you have to be confrontational or aggressive. It's about reclaiming your narrative, grounding yourself in your worth, and responding with grace and conviction. Here are some strategies and scripts to guide you:

1. Acknowledge, Don't Absorb:

Before formulating a response, internally acknowledge the comment without absorbing its negativity. Tell yourself, "This isn't about me. It's about their perception."

- Script: "I understand that's how you see it, but I have a different perspective."

2. The Power of "I" Statements:

Shift the focus from blame to expressing how you feel. This approach is less confrontational and opens up dialogue.

- Script: "I feel hurt when comments like that are made. I'd appreciate it if we could communicate more respectfully."

3. Assertive, Not Aggressive:

Stand your ground without being combative. You can assert yourself while maintaining respect.

- Script: "I don't agree with that. Let's discuss this calmly or revisit it later."

4. Ask Open-Ended Questions:

Sometimes, putting the ball back in their court can be powerful. It prompts reflection and potentially diffuses tension.

- Script: "Why do you feel that way?" or "What makes you say that?"

5. Set Immediate Boundaries:

If a comment or behavior crosses a line, it's crucial to establish boundaries then and there.

- Script: "I'm not comfortable with this topic. Let's discuss something else."

6. The Art of Deflection:

Sometimes, humor or changing the subject can be a useful tool, especially if you're not in the mood for confrontation.

- Script: "Well, every family needs an 'odd one' to keep things interesting!" or "Speaking of which, have you tried this delicious potato salad?"

7. Seeking Allies:

If someone else in the family understands or has been supportive, subtly drawing them into the conversation can diffuse scapegoating attempts.

- Script: "Actually, I was discussing this with [supportive family member], and we both feel..."

8. Choosing Silence:

Not every comment warrants a response. Sometimes, the most empowering thing is to not engage, showing that you're unbothered by baseless remarks.

Incorporating these strategies won't just challenge the scapegoat narrative but will also reinforce your self-worth. Over time, as you consistently respond with assertiveness and grace, the dynamics will start to shift. Remember, it's not about winning an argument; it's about standing in your truth. As we proceed, we'll delve into another vital aspect of self-empowerment: understanding and setting boundaries.

Imagine for a moment that your heart, your emotions, and your mental state reside within a beautiful, lush garden. This garden is your sanctuary, a place of peace and self-reflection. Now, what would happen if you left the gates of this garden wide open, allowing anyone and everyone to enter and trample over its delicate flowers? Over time, the beauty and serenity of your garden would be destroyed, its vibrant colors replaced by the chaos of footprints.

This garden is a metaphor for our emotional and mental space, and the boundaries we set are the protective walls and gates that keep it thriving.

Boundaries, simply put, are the invisible lines we draw around ourselves to maintain our well-being. They serve as guidelines for how we want to be treated, what we're willing to accept, and where we draw the line. Whether in friendships, romantic relationships, or familial ties, they are integral to preserving our emotional health.

Here's why boundaries are paramount:

1. Self-Preservation: Just as our physical body needs a barrier in the form of skin to protect our internal organs, our emotional self requires boundaries to protect our inner peace.

2. Fostering Mutual Respect: When boundaries are established and respected, they cultivate mutual admiration and understanding, paving the way for healthier interactions.

3. Preventing Burnout: By defining our limits, we ensure that we don't spread ourselves too thin or give more than we can afford to, emotionally or mentally.

4. Strengthening Self-Esteem: By setting boundaries, we affirm our self-worth. We send a clear message that we value ourselves enough to stand up for our well-being.

5. Creating Authentic Relationships: With clear boundaries, relationships are built on genuine understanding and respect rather than assumptions or impositions.

6. Enhancing Personal Growth: Recognizing and defining our boundaries helps us better understand ourselves, our needs, and our limits, fostering personal development.

The idea of setting boundaries can seem daunting, especially when it's with family members who've known you for a lifetime. It's not about creating barriers or shutting people out, but rather about crafting a space where you can thrive and have mutual respect. In the next segment, we'll discuss how to effectively establish and communicate these boundaries with loved ones.

We all have our breaking points, lines that shouldn't be crossed, and domains we hold dear. But how do we go about laying down the law, especially in a family setting where rules have often been implicitly set for decades? Here's a roadmap to help you define, communicate, and enforce your boundaries:

1. Self-Assessment and Reflection:

Start by examining your feelings and past experiences. Which family interactions leave you drained, disrespected, or overwhelmed? Pinpoint moments when you've thought,

"I wish they wouldn't do that." These feelings are indicators of where boundaries may be needed.

2. Be Clear and Specific:

Vagueness is the enemy of effective boundaries. Instead of saying, "I wish you'd respect my choices," specify what that respect looks like: "I'd appreciate it if you didn't make negative comments about my career decisions."

3. Communicate Calmly and Assertively:

Approach the topic when you're calm and choose a good time for the other person too. Use "I" statements to express how you feel and what you need, which focuses on your feelings rather than blaming them. For instance, "I feel overwhelmed when everyone seeks my advice simultaneously. I'd appreciate it if we could discuss issues one at a time."

4. Consistency is Key:

The more consistent you are in maintaining your boundaries, the clearer the message you send. If you give in occasionally, it sends mixed signals, making it harder for others to understand and respect your limits.

5. Be Prepared for Pushback:

Not everyone will respond positively when you first establish your boundaries. Some family members might be taken aback or even feel hurt. While this can be challenging, remember that it's a sign you're making necessary changes.

6. Use Non-Verbal Cues:

Sometimes, a firm but gentle gesture, like holding up your hand or taking a step back, can reinforce a verbal boundary.

7. Seek Support:

Discussing your boundaries with a supportive friend or therapist can provide validation. They might offer a different perspective or suggest ways to handle potential challenges.

8. Prioritize Your Well-being:

If a boundary is repeatedly ignored, consider limiting your interaction with the individual or seeking mediation. Remember, boundaries are about preserving your mental and emotional well-being.

9. Regularly Reassess:

As you grow and evolve, your boundaries might as well. It's okay to adjust them based on your current needs and circumstances.

10. Celebrate Small Wins:

Every time you successfully establish a boundary, acknowledge your effort. Whether it's taking a moment for yourself or discussing it with someone you trust, celebrate the steps you take toward a healthier, happier you.

Boundaries are more than just rules or barriers; they're a declaration of self-respect and an investment in your emotional health. As you embark on this journey of defining and defending your boundaries, remember that it's a continuous process, and every step forward is a victory.

In an ideal world, setting boundaries would be met with understanding and respect. However, reality often presents a different scenario, especially within families that may not be used to such limits. Guilt and manipulation can emerge as powerful tools to dissuade or discredit your efforts. This section will shed light on these challenges and offer strategies to navigate these treacherous waters.

Understanding the Source of Guilt:

Guilt, in this context, is often a byproduct of years of conditioning. Family, being our primary social unit, heavily influences our beliefs, values, and behaviors. When you begin to establish boundaries, it might feel like you're going against this ingrained programming, leading to feelings of guilt. Recognize that this guilt is not a testament to wrongdoing on your part, but rather an emotional response to change.

Accusations of Selfishness:

When you start setting boundaries, you might be met with resistance. Phrases like "you're being selfish" or "you've changed" can be thrown around. Understand that these are defense mechanisms. When one person starts to change the dynamics, it can unsettle others, leading them to use such tactics to restore the old equilibrium.

Strategies to Navigate Emotional Manipulation:

1. Stay Firm in Your Convictions: Remember why you're setting these boundaries in the first place. Reaffirming the reasons can provide the necessary strength to stand firm.

2. Avoid Over-Explaining: While it's important to communicate your boundaries clearly, avoid the trap of over-justifying. This can make it seem like you're seeking approval rather than stating your needs.

3. Practice Self-compassion: Be gentle with yourself. Recognize that guilt is a natural emotion, especially when changing long-standing dynamics. It doesn't mean you're in the wrong.

4. Seek External Support: Talk to friends, join a support group, or see a therapist. They can provide validation and different perspectives when navigating the emotional labyrinth of family dynamics.

5. Reframe the Narrative: Instead of viewing it as "being selfish," see it as "self-preservation" or "self-respect." This subtle change can make a big difference in how you perceive and feel about your actions.

6. Distance Yourself Temporarily: If the emotional manipulation becomes too much, it might be helpful to distance yourself for a short period. This can give you the space to regroup and approach the situation with a clearer mind.

7. Educate and Share: Sometimes, family members genuinely might not understand the concept of boundaries. Sharing articles, books, or even personal stories can be enlightening for them.

8. Stay Calm and Neutral: When faced with accusations or attempts at manipulation, respond calmly without getting defensive. Often, a measured response can defuse a volatile situation.

Navigating guilt and emotional manipulation can be one of the most challenging parts of setting boundaries. However, remember that these are often fleeting obstacles on the road to healthier relationships and a more balanced life. By staying true to yourself and equipped with these strategies, you can pave the way for more genuine connections, free from undue emotional burdens.

Just as an actor might rely on a script to navigate a performance, many of us unconsciously rely on scripts that have been handed down to us within our family structures. These scripts dictate roles, behaviors, and responses, becoming the lens through which we view our family relationships and, often, ourselves. For the scapegoat, this script can be particularly limiting, painting a picture of blame, dysfunction, or inadequacy. However, it's essential to remember that scripts can be rewritten. Here's how:

1. Recognize the Existence of a Script:

The first step in any transformative process is awareness. Understand that many family dynamics are based on patterns and narratives that have evolved over time. These are not absolutes but rather learned behaviors and beliefs.

2. Reflect on the Script's Origin:

Where did these narratives originate? Was it from a particular family member's beliefs or perhaps a response to certain events in the family's history? Understanding the origin can offer clarity and even empathy towards those who perpetuate these narratives.

3. Identify Harmful Narratives:

List down the recurring themes or statements that have been associated with your role as the scapegoat. These might include beliefs like "You're always the problematic one" or "You can't do anything right." Recognizing them is essential to challenging them.

4. Actively Counter Negative Perceptions:

When confronted with these old narratives, either internally or from family members, actively challenge them. This doesn't always mean a verbal confrontation. It can be as simple as reframing the narrative in your mind or showcasing through actions that you don't conform to the limiting beliefs.

5. Create a New Narrative:

What would you like your family story to be? This doesn't mean fabricating a reality, but focusing on strengths, positive interactions, and shifting away from the scapegoat label. Begin by visualizing positive interactions and gradually integrating these beliefs into your conversations and behaviors.

6. Reinforce the New Script:

Just as the old script was reinforced through repetition, the new narrative will need reinforcement. This might involve consistently asserting your new identity, setting boundaries, or seeking validation outside the family until the new narrative takes hold within it.

7. Seek Professional Guidance:

A therapist or counselor can provide valuable insights into the family dynamics and offer tools and strategies to help rewrite these ingrained scripts.

Changing old scripts is a journey, not a destination. It requires persistence, patience, and belief in one's capacity to redefine their role. Over time, with effort and consistency, it's possible to shift the narrative, not only in how the family perceives the scapegoat but in how the scapegoat perceives themselves. Remember, you are the author of your life's story, and you have every right to choose its direction and tone.

Engaging with family dynamics, especially when challenging a longstanding role like that of the scapegoat, can sometimes feel like navigating a minefield. It's all too easy to get ensnared in every dispute or negative comment that comes your way. Yet, it's essential to realize that not all battles are worth fighting. Choosing when to engage and when to step back is a crucial skill in preserving one's emotional health and ensuring meaningful change. Here's how to do it:

1. Assess Personal Importance:

When an issue arises, ask yourself: "Is this important to me? Does it align with my core values? Will it matter in a week, a month, or a year?" By discerning its significance in the grander scheme of your life, you can better decide if it's worth your energy.

2. Determine Potential Outcomes:

Before diving into a confrontation, it can be helpful to anticipate possible outcomes. Will the discussion lead to a productive outcome, or will it spiral into an unproductive and hurtful dispute?

3. Understand Emotional Triggers:

Be aware of topics or comments that hit a nerve. Recognizing these can help you approach such subjects with caution, preparedness, or sometimes, choosing to avoid them altogether for your peace of mind.

4. Practice Emotional Detachment:

Not every comment or critique warrants a visceral emotional reaction. Learning to detach emotionally from certain situations allows you to respond with clarity and avoid unnecessary confrontations.

5. Value Your Peace:

Sometimes, the best approach is to remain silent. Silence can be a powerful tool, signaling that you no longer engage in destructive dynamics. It's okay to prioritize your peace over the need to be right or validated.

6. Utilize Tactical Retreat:

If a situation becomes too heated or emotionally charged, give yourself permission to step back. It's okay to say, "I need a moment" or "Let's discuss this later."

7. Seek Outside Perspective:

Sometimes, an objective viewpoint can offer clarity. Discussing family issues with a trusted friend or therapist can provide insights into which battles are worth engaging in and which are better left untouched.

8. Embrace Forgiveness and Letting Go:

Understand that holding onto every grievance can be draining. Embrace the power of forgiveness, not necessarily because the other party deserves it, but because you deserve peace.

In the quest to redefine one's role within the family and to challenge the scapegoat label, it's essential to move with wisdom. Remember, every battle fought doesn't necessarily bring you closer to peace or validation. Sometimes, the most profound victories lie in the battles we choose not to engage in, allowing us to channel our energy towards healing, growth, and forging healthier relationships.

Amidst the intricate web of family dynamics, it's not uncommon to find pockets of understanding and empathy. These are family members who, even if they don't fully grasp the depth of the scapegoating process, sense the imbalance and display a readiness to support and connect on a deeper level. Building alliances within the family can be a pivotal strategy in your journey towards transformation. These alliances can offer emotional support, validation, and even act as mediators in challenging situations. Here's how to approach this:

1. Identify Potential Allies:

Reflect on your interactions with family members. Who listens without judgment? Who has shown signs of understanding or even shared their reservations about certain family dynamics? These individuals might be your potential allies.

2. Foster One-on-One Relationships:

Strengthening individual relationships outside of larger family gatherings can be beneficial. Spend time with these family members, sharing experiences, understanding their perspectives, and building trust.

3. Communicate Your Feelings:

Open up about your feelings and experiences with these empathetic family members. Use "I" statements to express your emotions, ensuring that you're not placing blame but seeking understanding.

4. Seek Feedback:

Sometimes, these family members can provide insights into family dynamics that you might not have noticed. Their external perspective can be invaluable in understanding complex interactions.

5. Respect Confidentiality:

If a family member confides in you or supports you privately, ensure you respect their wish to keep things confidential. Pushing them to take a stand before they're ready can strain the alliance.

6. Collaborate on Solutions:

Your allies might have suggestions or strategies for dealing with specific family members or situations. Collaborate and brainstorm on ways to address scapegoating behaviors or other challenging dynamics.

7. Understand Their Position:

Remember, while they're empathetic and supportive, they too have their relationship dynamics and challenges within the family. Be sensitive to their position and understand if there are times they cannot be as vocal or confrontational as you might wish.

8. Celebrate Small Wins:

Every time an ally stands up for you, validates your feelings, or even just listens, take a moment to appreciate it. These small wins, these moments of connection, can be deeply healing.

Building alliances isn't about creating a divide in the family or choosing sides. It's about recognizing that, within every family, there are members who are more receptive, understanding, and willing to challenge harmful dynamics. Connecting with these individuals can provide the emotional sustenance you need, making your journey towards healing and transformation a collective effort rather than an isolated struggle.

As you begin to challenge the long-established scapegoat role within your family, it's important to brace yourself for potential backlash. This resistance is often a natural reaction to change, especially when it disrupts a family's status quo. While the journey towards reclaiming your self-worth is incredibly empowering, the path might be strewn with obstacles, particularly in the form of intensified scapegoating or resistance from family members unprepared for change. Here's how to understand and navigate this backlash:

1. Anticipate Resistance:

Understand that not everyone will be supportive of your newfound assertiveness or the boundaries you set. Some family members may see it as an affront or challenge to the established order.

2. Recognize Intensified Scapegoating:

In an effort to maintain the status quo, there might be attempts to further label, blame, or isolate you. This is often a sign that your efforts are disrupting the harmful dynamic, even if it feels like things are getting worse.

3. Stay Grounded:

Hold onto your self-worth and the progress you've made. Remember your reasons for challenging the scapegoat role. Revisit the tools of self-awareness and reflection to remind yourself of your worth and purpose.

4. Rely on Your Support System:

Reach out to external sources of support, be it therapy, support groups, or trusted friends. Share your experiences and seek validation when faced with intense backlash.

5. Avoid Escalation:

While it's essential to stand up for yourself, choose your battles wisely. Not every comment or action warrants a response. Prioritize your emotional well-being.

6. Reaffirm Boundaries:

If family members test or cross the boundaries you've set, gently but firmly reaffirm them. Consistency is key to making these boundaries respected and recognized.

7. Reflect on Relationship Viability:

In extreme cases, where backlash becomes toxic, consider the possibility of limited contact or distance from particularly harmful family members. Your mental and emotional well-being should always be a priority.

8. Empower Yourself with Knowledge:

Understand the psychology behind scapegoating and resistance to change. Recognizing that these reactions are often less about you and more about the family's dysfunction can be liberating.

9. Stay Compassionate:

Remember that family members entrenched in these dynamics might be acting out of their unresolved traumas and insecurities. While this doesn't excuse their behavior, compassion can help you approach situations with understanding rather than anger.

10. Celebrate Your Resilience:

Each time you successfully navigate backlash or any form of resistance, take a moment to recognize your growth, strength, and resilience.

While facing backlash can be challenging and painful, it's also an indication of the transformative journey you're on. It underscores the fact that you're actively challenging a harmful dynamic. With each hurdle you overcome, you move one step closer to a healthier relationship with your family and, more importantly, with yourself. Remember, in this journey of self-assertion and breaking free from the scapegoat label, you're not alone—seek support, stay informed, and prioritize your well-being above all.

The path to breaking free from the stifling confines of the scapegoat role is neither linear nor simple. It requires introspection, courage, resilience, and an unwavering belief in one's intrinsic worth. However, as we have journeyed through this chapter, it becomes evident that not only is this path navigable, but it is also filled with potential for profound personal growth and healing.

Challenging age-old family dynamics might feel daunting, yet it's a crucial step in reclaiming your narrative and reshaping your role within the family. Through cultivating self-awareness, we begin to understand our emotions and identify the triggers that have held us captive for so long. With effective communication, we can express our feelings without casting blame, fostering understanding and possibly even empathy from our loved ones.

The power of external perspectives—be it from therapists, support groups, or empathetic friends—cannot be over-stated. They offer validation, clarity, and sometimes, the very tools we need to dismantle the scapegoat label. As we arm ourselves with empowering responses, we not only challenge the established dynamic but emphasize our worth in the process.

Boundaries, both in understanding and enforcing them, act as protective barriers, ensuring our emotional well-being and self-preservation. And while setting them might invite guilt or accusations of selfishness, we are equipped to navigate such emotional manipulations, always remembering that our well-being is paramount.

Engaging with our family under this new light means challenging old scripts and narratives, choosing our battles wisely, building alliances with those who support our transformation, and being prepared for the inevitable backlash.

Yet, even amidst resistance, there lies immense potential. Potential to rewrite our stories, to connect with family in deeper, more meaningful ways, and to step away from the shadows of the scapegoat role into a space of understanding, love, and respect.

As we conclude this chapter, take a moment to reflect on your journey so far and envision the healthier relationships that lie ahead. Understand that change, especially within the complex tapestry of family dynamics, takes time. Be patient with yourself and your loved ones. Most importantly, prioritize your well-being, knowing that in doing so, you pave the way for genuine connection and healing. The journey is worth it, and so are you.

5

HEALING THE WOUNDS
JOURNEY TOWARDS WHOLENESS

In the quiet recesses of my heart, I remember the times when the weight of being the family scapegoat pressed heavily on my shoulders. If you're reading this chapter, it's likely you've felt that same weight, the heaviness of carrying blame, shame, and unmet expectations. It's a pain I wouldn't wish upon anyone, a deep wound that festers, silently eroding our sense of self and the melodies of our voices. Yet, I am here to tell you something profound: healing is not only possible but awaits you.

No matter how entrenched you feel in the scapegoat role, know that the journey of healing is a transformative one. A journey that isn't about erasing the past but learning from it, embracing it, and then rising above it. Every wound, every scar tells a story; but rather than being a tale of victimhood, it can become a testament to your resilience, growth, and indomitable spirit.

This chapter is a tribute to that journey, a roadmap designed to guide you out of the labyrinth of hurt and into the open fields of self-awareness, acceptance, and genuine healing. Let's embark on this path, one where you reclaim not just your identity but also the strength and cadence of your voice.

"Know thyself," proclaimed the ancient Greeks, etching the adage onto the Temple of Apollo at Delphi. Thousands of years later, that sentiment still holds profound wisdom. As someone who's been pigeonholed into the scapegoat role, I can't emphasize enough the importance of knowing oneself, particularly in navigating the often murky waters of family dynamics.

Self-awareness is the compass you need. It's the ability to tune in, with compassionate curiosity, to your feelings, reactions, and those sneaky triggers that might catapult you back into old patterns. Remember the times you felt an inexplicable surge of anger during a family gathering? Or the twinge of sadness when someone cracked a joke at your expense? These emotions, once viewed as random or baseless, often hold clues. By understanding them, you start to unravel the tapestry of past hurts, biases, and learned reactions. You start seeing the patterns and, more importantly, understanding why they exist.

However, self-awareness is not about indulging in a self-blame game or brooding over past slights. It's an empowered stance, one where you acknowledge your emotions without being enslaved by them. It's recognizing that while you can't change the past or control others' actions, you can control your reactions, your understanding, and your healing.

If the scapegoat role was an invisible cloak that others draped over you, self-awareness is the light that makes that cloak transparent. By recognizing its weight and texture, you can finally choose to shed it.

You ever try shoving a cat into a bath? It's a fiasco. The cat squirms, resists, and maybe even leaves you with a few scratches. In many ways, our relationship with our past, especially one marked by being the family scapegoat, can feel like trying to dunk that distressed kitty into water. We wriggle, we resist, we reject. But the more we fight our past, the tighter its grip becomes.

Acceptance, on the other hand, is like gently coaxing the cat, acknowledging its fears, and then deciding on the best course of action. Maybe the bath isn't the answer. Maybe it's a gentle wipe down or a change of environment. Similarly, acceptance doesn't mean resigning yourself to a life of hurt or giving past traumas a free pass. It's about acknowledging that the pain happened but refusing to let it set up camp in your future.

I remember those Sundays at family gatherings where the jibes and sarcastic comments, draped in the garb of 'family jokes,' would fly thick and fast. The sting was real. But over time, I realized that nursing that hurt wasn't helping. It was like rewatching a movie where I was the unintentional protagonist in a plot I never auditioned for.

Embracing acceptance was liberating. I came to terms with the fact that I was the scapegoat, not because of any fault of mine, but because of complex family dynamics that had been in play long before I arrived on the scene. And here's the thing: Acceptance is not a finish line; it's a continuous journey. It's choosing every day to say, "Yes, that happened. But it doesn't get to dictate my story anymore."

Imagine your life as a book. Being the scapegoat might be a few chapters, perhaps even a significant chunk of the narrative. But acceptance gives you the pen to write the upcoming chapters, ensuring that while the past might shape you, it certainly doesn't define you. The future? Well, that's a blank page waiting for your story. And trust me, it's one worth telling.

Ah, the power of the pen! Or, you know, the keyboard if you're more tech-inclined. There's something almost magical about putting words to paper, like pouring out little bits of your soul. Now, I can hear some of you groaning, "Emily, I'm no Shakespeare!" But here's the thing: journaling isn't about crafting poetic masterpieces; it's about unveiling your thoughts and giving them a space to breathe.

When I was in the thick of my scapegoat days, I often felt like a pressure cooker on the brink of bursting. Emotions swirled, questions nagged, and regrets loomed. That's when I stumbled upon the therapeutic world of journaling. It wasn't a planned venture; it started with scribbles on napkins, rants in forgotten notebooks, and even the occasional doodle. But, over time, I found clarity amidst the chaos.

So, why journaling? It's a judgment-free zone. Your journal won't scoff at your feelings or offer unsolicited advice. Instead, it provides a space for reflection, allowing you to process complex emotions and recognize recurring patterns in your life.

A few prompts to kickstart your journaling journey:

- **Today, I felt...** (Fill in the blank. Dive deep.
  Were you feeling joyous, melancholic, indifferent,
  hopeful? Be as descriptive as you want.)

- **A memory that's been on my mind lately is...** (It could be from childhood, last week, or even a dream. Describe it in vivid detail. What did it make you feel?)
- **The role of scapegoat in my family feels like...** (Visualize it. Is it a heavy cloak? A pair of shackles? An invisible barrier?)
- **When I think about my future, I envision...** (Dream big or dream small, there's no right or wrong. What's your ideal day? What are the feelings you want to cultivate?)
- **One thing I'd tell my younger self is...** (A nugget of wisdom, a word of caution, a promise of brighter days—what do you wish you could convey?)

Remember, there's no 'right' way to journal. Some days, it might be paragraphs upon paragraphs. Other days, a single word or sketch. It's your space, your rules. Through journaling, you're not just jotting down words; you're charting a journey—a journey towards understanding, acceptance, and eventual healing. And as you leaf through the pages over time, you'll see not just where you've been, but how far you've come.

Remember those old cartoons where a character would take one step forward, but it seemed the universe conspired for them to take two steps back? Yep, life can sometimes feel like you're starring in one of those episodes. But here's a twist: every step, no matter how small or shaky, is a victory in its own right.

You see, when navigating the labyrinthine world of healing, it's easy to feel disheartened when the end seems distant or the "big" milestones appear unreachable. And that's why the power of small victories becomes paramount. They're the tiny bursts of light on a path that, at times, can feel overwhelmingly dark.

Now, what do I mean by "small" victories? Well, for someone, it could be the act of waking up and choosing to face another day, even with a heavy heart. For another, it might be as simple as speaking up when they'd normally remain silent or setting a boundary with a family member. It's the little moments when you recognize a past trigger but respond differently, when you choose love over resentment, or when you simply acknowledge the pain without letting it consume you.

To celebrate these moments, consider these simple practices:

1. **Victory Jar:** Get yourself a jar (or a box, or a bowl—anything, really). Every time you recognize a small victory, write it down on a piece of paper and pop it in. Over time, you'll have a tangible testament to your progress. On tough days, pull out a note and remind yourself of your journey.

2. **Daily Reflection:** Before you hit the sheets, take a moment to reflect on your day. Identify at least one thing, however minor, that you felt good about. Maybe you practiced self-care, or maybe you finally journaled after weeks of postponing. Cherish it.

3. **Share with a Trusted Ally:** If you have a friend or a support group, share your victories with them. There's something affirming about vocalizing your progress and receiving validation.

4. **Treat Yourself:** Who says you need a grand reason for a little treat? Enjoyed a peaceful morning without diving into past regrets? Have a cookie. Stood up for yourself in a small way? Maybe it's time for that book you've been eyeing.

Here's the deal: every victory, no matter how small, is a defiant act against the forces that once held you down. It's a proclamation that you're not just surviving; you're evolving. By celebrating the small stuff, you're not trivializing your journey; you're acknowledging that every step, every moment of growth, is an integral part of your grand narrative. So, my friend, give yourself the applause you deserve. Your journey, with all its ups and downs, is nothing short of spectacular.

While understanding and cultivating self-awareness lays the groundwork for healing, therapy offers structured avenues to directly confront and dismantle long-held negative beliefs. The pain and self-doubt associated with being scapegoated can be deeply rooted, often requiring specialized techniques to effectively address. One of the most potent tools in this endeavor, renowned for its efficacy in challenging distorted self-perceptions, is Cognitive Behavioral Therapy.

Cognitive Behavioral Therapy, often abbreviated as CBT, is a therapeutic approach grounded in the interconnection between thoughts, emotions, and behaviors. It operates on the premise that by identifying and challenging maladaptive thought patterns, we can transform our emotional responses and the consequent behaviors.

For those who've played the scapegoat role, negative self-perceptions may have become deeply entrenched. Thoughts like "I am the problem," "Nothing I do is right," or "I don't deserve love or respect" might be all too familiar. These negative thought patterns, developed over years of being unjustly blamed or marginalized, can lead to feelings of worthlessness, anxiety, or depression. Behaviorally, this might manifest as withdrawal from social situations, self-sabotage, or even engaging in relationships that mirror the dysfunctional dynamics of the past.

Here's where CBT steps in:

1. Identification: The first phase of CBT is about becoming aware. With the guidance of a therapist, you'll learn to pinpoint these automatic negative thoughts when they occur.

2. Challenge: Once these patterns are identified, the next step is to challenge their validity. For instance, just because you've been blamed doesn't mean you're inherently flawed. A therapist will guide you in interrogating these thoughts, looking for evidence, and weighing them against reality.

3. Replacement: After challenging the negative cognitions, you'll work on developing more balanced and positive replacements. Instead of "I am always wrong," a new thought might be "I have the right to my perspective, and I can learn from my experiences."

4. Behavioral Experiments: With new thought patterns in development, CBT often involves setting up real-life "experiments" to test out these beliefs and reinforce positive behaviors. For a scapegoat, this might mean practicing assertiveness or seeking out environments where their voice is valued and heard.

CBT is a collaborative process, one that necessitates an open dialogue between the therapist and the individual. It is particularly powerful for scapegoats because it offers tangible tools and strategies to dismantle the harmful narratives they've internalized. Over time, through consistent practice and reflection, individuals can break free from the chains of scapegoating and step into a more empowered, authentic self-concept.

The intricate tapestry of family dynamics can sometimes entangle individuals in experiences that go beyond the regular strains of misunderstandings and disagreements. For those who've undergone traumatic events within their family framework, memories can linger, often replaying vividly and disruptively in their minds. That's where EMDR comes into play.

EMDR, a therapeutic approach founded by Francine Shapiro, is specifically designed to address traumatic memories and alleviate the distress they cause. How does it work? Imagine a splinter lodged under your skin. It causes persistent pain until it's finally removed, after which the healing truly begins. Similarly, EMDR helps in processing those "splintered" traumatic memories, allowing them to be integrated appropriately so they no longer cause disproportionate distress.

The process itself is unique. During EMDR sessions, the therapist facilitates a structured set of bilateral eye movements (or other bilateral stimuli like hand taps or audio tones) while the individual recalls the traumatic event. These eye movements are believed to mimic the rapid eye movement (REM) stage of sleep, which plays a role in processing daily emotional experiences. Over time and with structured sessions, the emotional charge linked with the traumatic memory tends to diminish, often resulting in increased insight and resilience.

For scapegoats, especially those whose roles were solidified through traumatic events or repeated emotional or psychological abuses, EMDR can offer profound relief. It's as if one's mental photo album, previously filled with haunting images, gets a chance to be revisited, rescripted, and reorganized, paving the way for a future that's not overshadowed by the past.

Remember those times when you felt truly understood by someone? The relief of realizing, "I'm not alone in this?" Multiply that soothing realization by a group of empathetic listeners, and you begin to understand the power of group therapy and support groups.

Being a family scapegoat can feel incredibly isolating. It's like being caught in a storm while everyone else seems to be enjoying a sunny day. But stepping into a room, either physically or virtually, where others have weathered the same tempests can be game-changing.

Group therapy, facilitated by trained therapists, provides a structured environment where members can openly discuss their feelings, challenges, and progress. It's a place where shared experiences create mutual understanding. There's also a unique dynamic at play: observing and interacting with others in similar shoes can offer fresh perspectives on one's own challenges. As the group tackles issues together, they often discover collective wisdom and varied strategies to cope, heal, and thrive.

Support groups, while typically not led by professional therapists, offer their own unique brand of healing. They are communities of individuals who've walked similar paths. The sheer act of sharing one's story and hearing others echo similar sentiments brings validation. It whispers the comforting truth: "You're not imagining things. You're not overreacting. And you are certainly not alone."

In the context of family dynamics, these groups can play a pivotal role. They help dismantle the feelings of isolation and 'otherness' that many scapegoats wrestle with. Moreover, they foster a sense of belonging and understanding that might have been missing from one's familial interactions.

As the old saying goes, "Shared pain is half the pain, while shared joy is double the joy." In the company of those who truly 'get it,' both the shadows of the past and the hopeful rays of the future find their rightful place.

Amidst the tumult of memories, emotions, and societal expectations, there exists a sanctuary of stillness within each of us. That sanctuary is accessed through the doors of mindfulness and meditation, two practices that, while ancient, have found profound relevance in our modern quest for healing and self-understanding.

Mindfulness can be understood as the art of being present. It is the practice of observing our thoughts, feelings, and sensations without judgment, allowing us to stay anchored in the present moment. For the scapegoat, the mind can often be a whirlwind of past accusations, painful memories, and anticipatory anxieties about future conflicts. By practicing mindfulness, one learns to observe these thoughts without getting entangled in them. This detachment offers a clarity, enabling one to recognize patterns, triggers, and emotional reactions that may have previously gone unnoticed.

Several daily activities, such as mindful eating, mindful walking, or simply being aware of one's breath, can serve as gateways into this practice. Over time, mindfulness fosters a compassionate self-awareness, allowing individuals to meet their past pains with understanding rather than resentment.

Meditation, often seen as a sister practice to mindfulness, delves deeper into the realms of the inner self. It's akin to a quiet, deliberate journey inward, offering solace from the external chaos. Meditation practices, varying from focused breathwork to guided visualizations, have shown remarkable efficacy in reducing stress, anxiety, and depressive symptoms—common accompaniments of the scapegoat experience. Moreover, as one meditates regularly, there's an enhancement of the brain's plasticity, promoting emotional regulation, improved concentration, and a heightened sense of well-being.

For someone who has felt adrift, unanchored by the very family that should have been their haven, mindfulness and meditation act as the roots that reconnect them to the grounding essence of their being. They are tools, not just for healing but for rediscovery—a journey from the external turbulence to the internal oasis of peace.

From the outside, my family seemed the epitome of unity and perfection. Our living room walls showcased portraits that painted us as a joyous, tight-knit bunch. But those photos, I've come to realize, are mere snapshots, unable to capture the depth and complexities of daily life.

Growing up, I felt like an outsider in my own home. Sandwiched between Jack, the star athlete, and Lucy, the prodigious musician, I constantly found myself drowning in their larger-than-life shadows. Their achievements were the talk of our home, their stories retold with pride, while my tales and triumphs were often sidelined or, worse, ignored.

However, it wasn't just about the accolades. Whenever I tried to voice a dissenting opinion, share a concern, or even just express a feeling, I was met with dismissal. "You're just being sensitive," was the refrain I heard so often from my mother. Those words, intended or not, diminished my feelings, making me doubt my own experiences. Over time, whenever conflicts arose, I became the family's default scapegoat, shouldering blame even for issues I had no part in.

To avoid confrontations and further heartache, I withdrew into myself, speaking sparingly and treading carefully to avoid any potential triggers. Books became my refuge, and writing, my solace. On paper, I felt a freedom I couldn't find in my reality—a space where my voice mattered, where I could shout, argue, and express without fear.

Yet, despite this outlet, the weight of the silence I was forced into was stifling, a constant reminder of my supposed inconsequence in the family dynamic.

Growing up, I never really questioned the role I was cast into; it was as if I had been given a script I never auditioned for. Days turned into weeks, weeks into months, and I became proficient in playing my part. But everything changed one cool autumn evening.

I was attending a friend's book club, an oasis of sorts where we would escape from the worries of the world. That day, the discussion revolved around a memoir of a woman who had been the 'black sheep' of her family. As the pages turned and her story unfolded, it felt eerily like looking into a mirror. Every word, every emotion echoed my own experiences. It was as if the universe conspired for me to be there, at that exact moment, to hear that exact story.

The weight of realization hit hard. I wasn't alone in this. This wasn't just "how families are." It wasn't my imagination, and it wasn't something I had to accept. The tears streamed not just from the resonance of the story, but from the overwhelming mix of relief and rage. Relief, because I wasn't alone; rage, because of the years I had lost, suppressing my true self.

That night, I lay awake, wrestling with a whirlpool of emotions. But above the cacophony, a singular, powerful thought emerged: I didn't want to be trapped in this narrative anymore. The script wasn't written for me; it was thrust upon me. And it was time to write my own story. This profound realization became my compass, guiding me to seek therapy, confront my past, and set the stage for my healing journey.

Embarking on the path to healing wasn't linear; it was filled with trials, tribulations, and profound insights. My first step was seeking therapy, an avenue I hadn't previously considered. The idea of opening up my deepest wounds to a stranger felt both intimidating and vulnerable. But I knew that to heal, I had to confront the pain that lay buried deep within.

Finding the right therapist was a journey in itself. The first one I approached seemed distant, making me feel like just another case study. The second was kind but seemed to lack the depth of understanding I sought. But with the third therapist, Dr. Lorraine, something just clicked. Her gentle demeanor and compassionate approach created a safe space for me to unravel the layers of my past.

During our sessions, we delved deep into my childhood memories, tracing the patterns and behaviors that led to my role as the family scapegoat. There were sessions filled with tears, anger, and moments where the pain felt too raw to confront. But Dr. Lorraine was a beacon of support, guiding me through the murkiness of suppressed emotions, helping me process and understand them.

As the weeks turned into months, the fog began to lift. With each session, I learned to challenge the deeply ingrained beliefs about myself that I had held onto for years. I realized that I had internalized the negativity and criticisms thrown at me, which had shaped my self-worth. With Dr. Lorraine's guidance, I learned to separate my intrinsic value from the role I had been forced into.

A major breakthrough came when I confronted my family about my feelings and experiences. While it didn't result in the ideal family reunion, it was liberating. Speaking my truth, voicing out years of pent-up emotions, was cathartic. Not everyone understood or acknowledged their role, but that didn't matter as much anymore. For once, I stood up for myself, breaking free from the chains of the past.

Throughout this healing process, I discovered tools and techniques that became my anchor. Mindfulness practices, journaling, and joining a support group were instrumental in my recovery. Sharing my experiences with others, hearing their stories, and realizing the universality of such pain added another layer to my healing.

In this intricate dance of healing, there were missteps, backward tumbles, but most importantly, there were leaps of progress, hope, and self-discovery.

The silence that once consumed me began to dissipate, replaced by the burgeoning sound of my own voice. A voice that had for so long been stifled, questioned, and overshadowed was now strong, clear, and unwavering. This wasn't just about speaking up, but about understanding the value of what I had to say and recognizing that my voice mattered.

I began to engage in conversations with conviction, no longer second-guessing every word or fearing criticism. Conversations with family became more authentic, as I learned the art of setting boundaries and expressing my feelings without seeking validation. With friends and colleagues, I took on leadership roles, shared my experiences, and advocated for those who still felt voiceless.

My newfound confidence allowed me to explore avenues I hadn't before. I took up public speaking, sharing my story at seminars and workshops, aiming to inspire and guide others on their journey of self-discovery. Writing became a therapeutic outlet, and soon, articles and essays flowed from my pen, chronicling my journey and the insights gleaned along the way.

Looking in the mirror, I no longer saw the downtrodden scapegoat, but a resilient individual who had weathered storms and emerged stronger. My past, with all its pain and challenges, became a testament to my strength, teaching me empathy, resilience, and the transformative power of self-acceptance.

As I moved forward, my mantra became clear: Our voices, once lost or suppressed, can be reclaimed. And when they are, they possess the power to heal, inspire, and change not just our own world, but the world around us. With my voice reclaimed, I was no longer just existing; I was truly living, speaking my truth, and making a difference, one word at a time.

The journey of the scapegoat, filled with challenges and heartaches, is undeniably a tumultuous one. But as we've traversed through this chapter, we've unearthed a profound truth: healing, though complex, is entirely within reach. Every step taken towards understanding oneself, every therapy session attended, every journal entry written, and every moment of self-awareness is a testament to the resilience of the human spirit.

Being scapegoated is not a life sentence, nor does it define the entirety of who you are. It's a chapter in your life story, one that can be followed by chapters of growth, empowerment, and self-discovery. The wounds inflicted upon you, though deep and painful, have the potential to be the very catalysts that propel you towards a journey of profound healing.

Remember, you are not alone in this journey. As you've seen from personal accounts and therapeutic insights, countless individuals have walked this path before you, facing similar struggles, and have emerged stronger and more attuned to their inner selves.

As we conclude this chapter, hold onto this unwavering truth: You deserve every ounce of love, respect, and understanding that the world has to offer. Your voice, muffled for so long, is waiting to resonate, to tell your story, and to assert your rightful place in the world. No matter how challenging the road ahead might seem, trust in your strength, believe in your worth, and know that a future where you speak your truth, unapologetically and boldly, awaits you.

6

_____

SELF-CARE AND SELF-LOVE
FILLING THE VOID

Imagine standing at the edge of a vast canyon. Its depths echo with the voices of past criticisms, misunderstandings, and emotional neglect, resonating with the coldness that often accompanies the role of the family scapegoat. Each negative word, each accusation, and each unfair expectation has carved this canyon deeper and wider. This, dear reader, is the void that many scapegoats come to know intimately— a gaping chasm in their hearts that, for years, has seemed insurmountable.

But what if I told you that this void, as daunting as it may appear, can be filled? Not with external validations, fleeting pleasures, or even the longed-for acceptance of family. No, it can be filled with something far more potent and transformative: self-love and self-care. These two elements, often overlooked in our relentless pursuit of external achievements and validations, are the very bedrock upon which we can rebuild ourselves.

In this chapter, we'll embark on a journey of introspection and self-nurturing, helping you recognize and embrace the beautiful potential within. Just as a river gradually fills a canyon, reshaping its contours and bringing life to its barrenness, so too can self-love and self-care replenish and reshape the void left by years of being the family scapegoat. Let's begin this transformative exploration, guiding you towards filling that void and reclaiming the vibrant soul that resides within.

When most people hear the term "self-care," their minds instantly wander to images of luxurious spa days, indulgent bubble baths, or tropical vacations. And while these delightful activities undoubtedly fall under the umbrella of self-care, they represent just the tip of a much more profound and transformative iceberg.

Self-care, in its true essence, is a holistic practice that goes beyond the superficialities of pampering. It's not about escapism or mere relaxation, though those can be lovely side effects. Instead, it's about actively tuning in, listening, and responding to your unique needs across every facet of your being.

Physical self-care, of course, is a pillar and includes nourishing your body with healthy foods, engaging in regular exercise, and ensuring adequate rest. It's about respecting your body's boundaries, understanding when to push and when to pull back.

But equally vital is mental self-care. This means allowing yourself the space to declutter your mind, whether it's through meditation, journaling, or simply taking regular breaks from the digital noise of our modern world. It's about continuously feeding your mind with positive affirmations, knowledge, and experiences that fuel growth.

Then there's emotional self-care, perhaps the most over-looked aspect, especially for scapegoats who've grown accustomed to suppressing their feelings. It involves validating your emotions, giving yourself permission to feel without judgment, and seeking emotional outlets, whether through therapy, art, or heartfelt conversations with trusted allies.

So, if you've been visualizing self-care as just a fleeting moment of indulgence, I invite you to expand that vision. See it as an ongoing, dynamic process that requires intention, commitment, and a keen understanding of oneself. It's about fostering a harmonious relationship with every part of you, ensuring that each aspect—physical, mental, and emotional—thrives in synchrony.

Picture yourself as a houseplant. Imagine if that plant was continuously moved from one corner of the room to the other, subjected to erratic watering, and occasionally placed in the dark. Over time, that plant would wither, its vibrant leaves turning brown, curling up in distress. But, with consistent care—appropriate sunlight, the right amount of water, and occasional words of encouragement (yes, plants love that!)—that same plant could revive, flourish, and blossom.

Similarly, being the scapegoat in a family is like being that neglected houseplant. The inconsistent treatment, the blame, the emotional darkness—these elements cast shadows over your sense of self, withering your spirit. Recovery from such deep-rooted trauma is not an overnight process, but a journey. And this is where the golden elixir of self-care comes in.

Consistent self-care serves as a balm for the wounds inflicted by years, or even decades, of scapegoating. Each act of care sends a powerful message to your subconscious: "I matter. My well-being is important." Over time, these repeated affirmations begin to counteract the internalized negative messages you've carried as a scapegoat.

By physically taking care of yourself, you rebuild the trust in your own body, often pushed to its limits by stress and emotional turmoil. The rush of endorphins from exercise, the healing touch of a massage, or the rejuvenating power of a full night's sleep—all these acts of physical self-care start mending the broken connection between the body and mind.

Mental self-care allows for the reprocessing and reframing of traumatic experiences. By giving yourself the space to reflect, to learn, and to grow, you challenge and ultimately change the narrative that was written for you. You begin to author your own story, one where you are not the perennial villain but the hero.

Emotionally, regular self-care rituals cultivate resilience. As you validate and honor your feelings, you learn not to run from them but to sit with them, understanding that they are transient. This emotional grounding and stability become essential tools in navigating triggers and moments of vulnerability in the recovery journey.

In essence, think of self-care as your anchor, keeping you grounded amidst the tumultuous seas of recovery. While the waves of past traumas might occasionally crash against you, with your anchor firmly planted, you'll remain steady, resilient, and on course toward healing.

Now, I know what you might be thinking: "Emily, I'm not exactly the 'bubble bath and candles' kind of person." And you know what? That's absolutely okay. True self-care is not about fitting into a one-size-fits-all mold. It's about understanding and responding to what *you* need in any given moment. It's the art of listening to yourself and asking, "What do I need right now?" And guess what? The answers might vary, and that's the beauty of it.

1. Physical Activity:

Let's start with something most of us have a love-hate relationship with: exercise. But hold on, I'm not asking you to sign up for a marathon (unless that's your jam). Here are some flexible options:

- Walking: Whether it's a brisk walk in the park or a leisurely stroll, walking is therapeutic. You could even make it meditative with some mindful walking.
- Yoga: This ancient practice is not just about flexibility; it's a connection between mind, body, and soul. Plus, there are countless YouTube tutorials for all levels.
- Dance: Put on your favorite tune and just let loose. It's liberating and an instant mood booster!

2. Relaxation Techniques:

The world can sometimes feel like it's set on 'fast forward'. It's crucial to hit the 'pause' button.

- Deep Breathing: Take a moment, close your eyes, and focus on your breath. Inhale deeply, hold, exhale. It's like a mini-reset for your body.
- Guided Imagery: Imagine your favorite place—be it a beach, a forest, or atop a mountain. Feel yourself there, soaking in the peace.
- Progressive Muscle Relaxation: Tense and relax your muscles systematically. It's surprisingly soothing.

3. Hobbies:

Remember those things you loved doing but then life got in the way? It's time to bring them back.

- Reading: Escape to another world, learn something new, or simply enjoy the beauty of words.
- Crafting: Be it knitting, painting, or DIY projects—creating something with your hands is incredibly satisfying.
- Music: Play an instrument, listen to a new album, or attend a local gig. Let music heal and elevate you.

4. Social Engagements:

While self-care often starts as a solitary journey, remember we're social creatures.

- Connect: Spend quality time with loved ones—those who uplift and understand you.

- Join a Group: Be it a book club, a hiking group, or a choir. Surrounding yourself with like-minded individuals can be affirming.
- Volunteer: There's something profound about giving back. It puts things into perspective and adds a sense of purpose.

Now, here's your homework: Grab a pen and paper, and jot down what resonates with you. Create your tailored self-care routine. And hey, it's okay to mix things up. Some days you might crave solitude, other days, company. Listen to yourself and adjust accordingly. Remember, this journey is uniquely yours.

While the journey of self-care illuminates the pathways to physical, emotional, and mental well-being, there's an even more profound inner journey that beckons: the journey of self-love. If self-care is the nourishing balm that soothes the external wounds, then self-love is the inner healing elixir that mends the deeper, often invisible scars. Particularly for those who've been relegated to the shadows as scapegoats, self-love isn't just an optional luxury; it's a lifeline, an essential antidote to the chronic neglect they've endured. As we transition from under-standing the myriad ways of nurturing our outer selves through self-care, let us dive deep into the sanctuary of our souls, discovering and embracing the transformative power of self-love.

At its core, self-love is a deliberate act of treating oneself with kindness, compassion, and understanding, much like how one would treat a loved one. However, in the landscape of modern pop psychology and personal growth, self-love can sometimes be misconstrued or over-simplified. So, let's delve deeper and clarify what it truly means.

Understanding Self-Love:

Self-love isn't merely about indulging oneself or being overly self-focused. Nor is it about inflating one's ego to unrealistic proportions. It's about truly understanding and appreciating oneself, both strengths and weaknesses. It's about recognizing one's intrinsic worth, irrespective of external validations or achievements.

Differentiating from Narcissism:

Narcissism and self-love might appear similar to an external observer, but they stem from entirely different roots. While both involve a strong focus on the self, the motivations and outcomes are diametrically opposite.

Narcissism is characterized by an inflated sense of importance, often at the expense of others. It's about seeking external validation and is fueled by a deep-seated insecurity. Narcissists often lack empathy and can even exploit others to satisfy their own needs or desires.

On the other hand, self-love comes from a place of genuine self-acceptance and understanding. It encourages empathy and understanding towards others because when one truly loves oneself, they recognize the same intrinsic worth in others. It's about filling one's own cup so that one can be of service to the world, not depleting others to fill a void.

Beyond Mere Self-Esteem:

Self-esteem, while valuable, is based on the evaluation of oneself, often in relation to achievements or in comparison to others. It's about "how well" one thinks of oneself. However, self-love transcends these evaluations.

Self-love persists even on days you might not feel particularly proud of your actions. It's a steady undercurrent, a continuous acknowledgment that you are deserving of love, respect, and understanding, not because of what you've achieved, but simply because you exist.

In essence, while self-esteem might ebb and flow based on life's circumstances, self-love remains a steadfast anchor.

As we navigate the intricacies of self-love, it's crucial to understand its transformative power, especially for those who've been chronically neglected or scapegoated. Embracing self-love can be the key to healing and rediscovering one's worth.

You know that empty, echoing sensation of walking into a derelict building? That's what years, sometimes decades, of neglect can make a person's soul feel like. The life of a scapegoat is often punctuated by those echoing moments — a lack of acknowledgment, consistent blame, or even deliberate invisibility within the family framework. It's an emotional drought where love, validation, and support are sporadically given or often withheld.

Neglect isn't always about overt cruelty or abuse. Sometimes, it's the silence, the omissions, the "forgotten" birthdays, or the constant comparison to others. It's that stinging realization that you're the last to be considered and the first to be blamed. The void created by this neglect isn't just an absence; it's a palpable presence, like a specter hovering in the peripheries of one's consciousness, reminding them of their purported unworthiness.

Now, let's talk about nourishment.

Nourishment, especially in the form of self-love, isn't just about filling that void. It's about transforming it. It's about recognizing that, despite the narrative the scapegoat has been given, they are deserving of love, from others and most importantly, from themselves. While neglect erodes the foundation of self-worth, self-love fortifies and rebuilds it.

Imagine your heart, for years parched and barren, suddenly feeling the life-giving drops of rain. That's what self-love does. It isn't a mere antidote; it's a reviving force. It's the understanding that your value isn't contingent on external validations or the roles others assign to you. Self-love is the whisper that grows into a confident voice, stating, "I am enough. I always have been."

The journey from neglect to nourishment is transformative. Where once stood a crumbling edifice of self-doubt now stands a rejuvenated monument of self-worth, reinforced by love, respect, and acceptance. And the beautiful thing? This transformation begins and blooms from within, untouched and unmarred by external opinions. This, dear reader, is the magic of self-love — a power that has always resided within you, waiting to be harnessed.

The journey to self-love isn't just about understanding its importance; it's about consciously integrating it into your daily life. To truly harness its transformative power, one needs to engage in practices that help embed this love deep within the fabric of their being. Below, we'll introduce a series of exercises designed to nurture and boost your self-love. Like any muscle, the more you work on it, the stronger it becomes. Let's delve into these practices:

1. Positive Affirmations:

- How: Begin your day by saying positive affirmations to yourself. These are powerful statements that help rewire negative thought patterns, replacing them with uplifting and empowering beliefs.
- Examples: "I am worthy of love and respect." "Every challenge I face is an opportunity for growth." "I trust the journey of my life."

2. Mirror Work:

- How: Stand in front of a mirror, looking directly into your own eyes. Speak words of love and affirmation to your reflection. This practice, pioneered by Louise Hay, confronts one's self-image and reinforces positive self-perception.
- Examples: "You are beautiful." "I love you, [Your Name]."

3. Gratitude Practices:

- How: Every night before sleeping, jot down three things you're grateful for about yourself. This shifts the focus from external factors to appreciating your own qualities, achievements, and growth.
- Examples: "I am grateful for my resilience in handling today's meeting." "I appreciate my kindness towards the barista this morning."

4. Self-Compassion Journal:

FROM FAMILY SCAPEGOAT TO SUMMIT

- How: Whenever you face a challenge or make a mistake, instead of spiraling into self-criticism, write a compassionate letter to yourself. Treat yourself as you would a dear friend.
- Examples: "It's okay to feel upset about the mistake, but remember one error doesn't define you. Learn and move forward."

5. Mindfulness and Meditation:

- How: Engage in regular mindfulness practices. By being present and fully engaging with the current moment, you cultivate a deep acceptance of yourself, warts and all. Meditation, especially loving-kindness meditation, can be powerful for fostering self-love.

6. Physical Nurturing:

- How: Engage in activities that make your body feel loved and cared for. This could be a massage, a warm bath, or even a simple act like moisturizing your skin. The key is to be present and do it with intent, acknowledging it as an act of love towards yourself.

7. Setting Achievable Goals:

- How: Every month, set small, achievable goals for yourself. When you accomplish them, it not only boosts your self-esteem but also reinforces your trust in your abilities.

- Examples: "This month, I'll read two books." "I'll practice ten minutes of meditation every morning."

By embedding these exercises into your routine, you're not just fostering self-love; you're also creating a protective shield against external negativity. Remember, the more you invest in understanding, accepting, and loving yourself, the more resilient and radiant you become.

Boundaries, often misunderstood as walls or barriers, are in fact bridges to better self-understanding and healthier relationships. They serve as clear demarcations of where one person ends and another begins. In the context of self-love, setting and maintaining boundaries is not just a beneficial act; it's a profound declaration of self-respect and self-worth.

1. The Essence of Boundaries: At its core, a boundary is a clear understanding and communication of what one is comfortable with, and what one is not. It is a line that marks the limits of acceptable behavior and interactions. Think of it as the property line around your house; it delineates what is yours and keeps out what could harm you.

2. The Connection to Self-Love: When you love someone, you aim to protect them, understand them, and prioritize their well-being. The same principle applies to self-love. By setting boundaries, you're safeguarding your mental, emotional, and physical space. You're asserting that you value your peace, energy, and time. It's an acknowledgment that you deserve respect and understanding, not just from others but, more importantly, from yourself.

3. Types of Boundaries:

- Emotional Boundaries: Protect your emotional space by recognizing and communicating your feelings. Do not allow others to dismiss, invalidate, or dump their emotions onto you without consent.
- Mental Boundaries: Guard your thoughts and values. Understand that you have the right to your own beliefs and opinions, and you shouldn't be coerced into adopting someone else's.
- Physical Boundaries: This relates to personal space and physical touch. Clearly communicate your comfort levels and ensure they are respected.
- Time Boundaries: Understand the value of your time. Ensure you allocate time for self-care, work, and other commitments in a balanced manner.

4. The Aftermath of Scapegoating: For someone who has lived the life of a scapegoat, boundaries might have been consistently breached. Over time, this can lead to a sense of powerlessness or a belief that one's desires and needs are irrelevant. But reclaiming the power to set and enforce boundaries can be a pivotal step in the healing process. It signals a move from victimhood to empowerment, from neglect to self-nurturing.

5. How to Set Boundaries:

- Self-awareness: Understand your needs, values, and limits. Reflect on past experiences where you felt discomfort or resentment due to breached boundaries.

- Clear Communication: Clearly, calmly, and assertively communicate your boundaries. Avoid being aggressive or passive-aggressive.
- Consistency: Once set, it's crucial to maintain and enforce these boundaries. This might involve reminding others (and yourself) occasionally.
- Reevaluation: As you grow and evolve, your boundaries might shift. Regularly reevaluate and adjust as necessary.

When it comes to loving yourself, boundaries are like the golden threads that hold it all together. They ensure that the fabric isn't torn apart by external pressures or internal turmoil. By setting boundaries, you're not pushing others away; you're inviting them to interact with you in a more genuine, respectful, and loving manner. Remember, boundaries aren't about keeping the world out but about ensuring you remain whole within it.

From the structured world of understanding self-love and setting boundaries, we venture into the more intimate, vulnerable realm of personal experience. Like a quiet corner of a bustling room, the story that unfolds provides a close-up of the effects of scapegoating on an individual's psyche. It's a journey not just of scars and shadows, but of redemption and rebirth.

In a home filled with the constant chatter of loved ones, it's paradoxical to feel an overwhelming sense of solitude. The laughter, the shared moments, the family dinners – from the outside, everything seemed picture-perfect. But within, a tempest of isolation raged.

Despite being surrounded by those who were supposed to be sources of comfort, an impenetrable bubble of loneliness enveloped me. Every conversation felt superficial, every interaction a mere transaction. It was as though I existed on a different frequency, where my feelings, thoughts, and voice couldn't breach the barrier to reach the others. The role of the family scapegoat left a stain on my identity, making me believe that perhaps, I was destined to be alone even in a crowd.

Even the simplest of misunderstandings were laid at my feet, the weight of unsaid expectations pressing down, creating a chasm between me and the rest of the family. Every side glance, every whispered conversation, I believed, was a testament to my perceived inadequacies. The more I felt misunderstood and isolated, the more I retreated, turning my back on the world outside and, tragically, on the world within.

The loneliness of being a scapegoat isn't just about feeling left out; it's a gnawing sense of being fundamentally flawed, of being perpetually out of sync with everyone else. This deep-rooted loneliness isn't merely the absence of company; it's the absence of genuine connection and understanding.

With time, the cocoon of isolation I had woven around myself began to shift from being a prison to a sanctuary. At first, solitude was a bitter pill, a constant reminder of my alienation. But slowly, as the outside noise dimmed, I began to hear the whispers of my own soul.

Solitude allowed me to turn inwards, away from the cacophony of judgments and misunderstandings that had played on a loop for so long. Within this newfound stillness, I began to ask myself questions that had long been buried under the rubble of external validation and familial expectations. Who am I, separate from the roles and labels assigned to me? What makes my spirit soar, my heart sing? What are the stories, desires, and dreams that live within me, waiting for an audience?

Rather than seeing solitude as an imposed exile, I began to view it as a journey to the most sacred destination: my inner self. I took up journaling, penning down my thoughts, fears, and aspirations. I read voraciously, finding solace in the experiences and wisdom of others who had walked paths similar to mine. I took long walks in nature, allowing the rhythmic cadence of my footsteps to become a meditative dance with the universe. Nature became a mirror, reflecting back my own innate resilience and capacity for growth.

Each day spent in solitude was akin to peeling back layers, shedding the accumulated burdens of years of misrepresentation and misconstrued identity. And as each layer fell away, I found pieces of myself that I hadn't known existed — fragments of joy, reservoirs of strength, and a deep well of compassion born from my own trials.

It wasn't an easy path. There were moments of doubt, times when the shadows of the past loomed large, threatening to swallow the progress I had made. But with every challenge faced, with every demon confronted, the light of self-awareness grew brighter, guiding me further along the path of self-discovery.

My foray into self-care began tentatively, fueled by the realization that if I didn't advocate for my well-being, no one else would. Initially, it was about simple acts: a warm bath, a few stolen moments with a book, or listening to soothing music. These small steps were my early attempts at soothing the raw, emotional wounds that scapegoating had inflicted upon me.

But as I deepened my relationship with solitude, my understanding of self-care evolved. It became less about occasional indulgences and more about establishing a consistent routine that prioritized my mental, emotional, and physical health. I explored yoga, finding solace in its harmonizing blend of movement and stillness. Meditation became a daily anchor, providing clarity amidst the internal storms.

Yet, as beneficial as these practices were, I recognized that true healing required more. It demanded self-love. No longer could I rely on external validations for my worth; I had to find it within myself. The journey was anything but linear. There were days when self-doubt was a loud critic, reminding me of all the voices that had belittled and dismissed me. But with each bout of uncertainty, I turned to affirmations. Whispered at first, then spoken with increasing confidence, these affirmations became the mantras that reshaped my self-image: "I am enough," "I am worthy of love and respect," "My experiences and feelings are valid."

Mirror work was particularly transformative. Looking into my own eyes, I would repeat these affirmations, forcing myself to confront the pain, the resilience, the hope, and the strength reflected back at me. Over time, the face in the mirror became a friend, an ally, a testament to my journey from neglect to self-acceptance.

The transformations were subtle but profound. The heaviness that once weighed down my spirit began to lift, replaced by a buoyancy I hadn't felt in years. I smiled more, not for others but for myself. I learned to celebrate small victories, like setting boundaries or vocalizing my needs. As I embraced self-love, my world began to shift. Relationships that were once strained started to heal, and opportunities that resonated with my true self began to appear.

The path was neither smooth nor straight, but every step, every stumble, became a testament to my commitment to love and care for the person I had neglected the most: myself.

As the days turned into months and the months into years, solitude transformed from an imposed exile to a chosen sanctuary. The quiet moments, once filled with the deafening echoes of past accusations and criticisms, became opportunities for deep introspection and reflection. It was within this silence that I began to truly hear, to listen to the whispers of my inner self that had been drowned out for so long.

Solitude taught me patience. It taught me to sit with discomfort, to acknowledge it, and to let it pass. It reminded me that healing is not a race, but a journey – one that requires time, space, and a lot of self-compassion. The stillness brought forth clarity, allowing me to sift through the external narratives that had been imposed upon me and discern my own truth from them.

My solitary rituals, whether they were morning meditations, evening journaling sessions, or solitary walks in nature, became the pillars of my daily life. They grounded me, providing a consistent space for self-reflection and growth. It was within these rituals that I discovered the nuances of my identity, the multifaceted nature of my being that went far beyond the limited role of a scapegoat.

And with every revelation, a newfound strength emerged. A strength that was not defiant or aggressive but calm and assertive. It was the strength of someone who had delved deep into the abyss of their psyche, faced their darkest fears, and emerged with a luminous understanding of their worth.

In embracing solitude, I didn't just find myself; I discovered a reservoir of resilience, wisdom, and love. A reservoir that had always been there, waiting to be tapped into. It became evident that solitude wasn't a punishment; it was a gift. A sacred space where one could shed old skins, birth new dreams, and emerge renewed. Through this journey, I learned that while the world might have its opinions and judgments, the most essential conversation is the one we have with ourselves, and it's within the sanctum of solitude that this dialogue finds its most profound depths.

As we draw this chapter to a close, the overarching theme that emerges is the transformational power of turning inward. The narratives, labels, and roles that have been thrust upon us, especially for those who have experienced the debilitating weight of being scapegoated, can leave scars. But those very scars bear testament to our resilience and capacity for growth.

Self-care and self-love are not mere buzzwords or passing trends. They are essential tools in the arsenal of anyone embarking on a journey of recovery and self-discovery. Just as a plant needs water, sunlight, and nourishment to flourish, our souls require care, attention, and love to truly thrive. This nurturing isn't an act of indulgence; it's an act of survival and revival.

As you progress in your journey, remember that every step you take toward self-care is a step away from the shadows of the past. Every act of self-love is a declaration of your worth, a reaffirmation that goes beyond the labels and roles that society or family might have assigned to you. It's an assertion that you matter, that your well-being is paramount, and that you are deserving of every drop of love and care you bestow upon yourself.

So, as you move forward, carry with you the lessons from this chapter. Prioritize your well-being. See your intrinsic worth. Remember, the narrative of your life is yours to pen, and every day presents a fresh page. As you write your story, let it be one of healing, growth, and unabashed self-love.

7

RECLAIMING YOUR LIFE AND PERSONAL POWER

EMERGING STRONGER FROM THE SHADOWS

Sunsets, though beautiful, signify an ending. But with every sunset, there's the hope of a sunrise. Similarly, having been cast into the shadows as the family scapegoat doesn't denote a lifelong sentence to darkness. It's the sunset before your brilliant sunrise. As we turn the page to this new chapter, we're not just learning how to emerge from the shadows but how to shine brighter than ever before. This chapter is your journey from the peripheries of your own story to center stage, a transformative process that burgeons with empowerment and personal growth. Let me take you, hand in hand, through this journey that I too once walked – from feeling powerless to celebrating the limitless strength within.

It's the promise of new beginnings, of reclaiming not just the narrative but the very essence of who you are. After all, when the world tried to bury us, little did they know we were seeds ready to grow. Let's embark on this journey of sprouting, flourishing, and reclaiming our life and personal power.

Coming up next: We'll delve into the core aspects of building resilience and self-esteem, the pillars that hold up our renewed sense of self. These aren't just terms thrown around in psychology textbooks. These are the foundations upon which we rebuild our lives. Let's lay down that first brick, shall we?

Imagine your mind as a magnificent mansion. Within it lie countless rooms filled with memories, dreams, fears, and aspirations. The foundation of this mansion is constructed from two fundamental elements: resilience and self-esteem. Without a robust foundation, even the grandest mansion can crumble in the face of a storm. Likewise, without resilience and self-esteem, our inner world can easily be swayed by external pressures.

Resilience is our innate ability to bounce back, to rise again after being pushed down, and to continue forward even when the path is strewn with obstacles. It's the rubber ball effect; no matter how hard you toss it to the ground, it bounces back. Think back to the times you've been side-lined, the moments you felt powerless, the pain of being the scapegoat. Yet, here you are, reading this, searching for a way out and forward. That, my friend, is resilience in action.

Self-esteem, on the other hand, is our self-worth, our belief in our own abilities and value. It's the whisper that tells you, "I am enough", even when the world tries to convince you otherwise. It's the fuel that drives our actions, the conviction behind our choices, and the shield against the critics, external or internal.

When resilience and self-esteem combine, they form an unbreakable bond, a force that not only helps us withstand life's tempests but allows us to thrive amidst them. They are the pillars upon which we build our inner strength, the guardians that shield our heart from hurt, and the compass that guides us towards self-fulfillment. As we venture further into this chapter, I'll take you on a deep dive into understanding, nurturing, and fortifying these essential cornerstones of our inner foundation. Ready to lay some bricks?

Let's begin with resilience. Resilience is like the unsung hero in an epic adventure movie. Quietly working behind the scenes, ensuring the protagonist keeps pushing forward, even when every odd is stacked against them. If life were a movie (and sometimes it sure feels like one, doesn't it?), resilience would be that unsung hero for many of us.

So, what is resilience, exactly?

At its core, resilience is the process of adapting well in the face of adversity, trauma, tragedy, or significant sources of stress. It's not about avoiding challenges or sidestepping difficulties; that's an entirely different ballgame (and not always a winning one). Resilience is about facing those challenges head-on and finding ways to come out stronger on the other side.

Imagine a willow tree during a storm. While the robust oaks and maples might snap under the force, the willow bends, sways, and then gracefully returns to its original form once the storm passes. That ability to "bend" without "breaking" embodies the essence of resilience.

Being the family scapegoat, as many of you know, is like facing an unending series of storms. The winds of blame, the rains of shame, and the thunder of unjust accusations can often feel overwhelming. But here's the silver lining: enduring such storms can also forge an incredible resilience within you. It's like strengthening a muscle – the more you exercise it, the stronger it becomes.

Now, this doesn't mean that resilient people don't experience distress or pain. Oh, they do! But they've developed the tools and mindsets to cope, recover, and often grow from these experiences. It's like having an internal GPS system that, even when thrown off course, recalibrates and finds a new path forward.

In the next segment, we'll delve into some of these tools and practices that can nurture and boost your resilience. Because, let's face it, while the storms of life are inevitable, how we weather them truly defines our journey.

Think of resilience as the magical rebounding ability that lets those squishy toys pop right back up, no matter how many times they're pushed over. But here's the kicker, we aren't born with an innate sense of this kind of springiness. It's cultivated, honed, and practiced. So, how do you train yourself to be one of those unstoppable, always-bouncing-back individuals? Here are some practical exercises to get you started:

1. Cognitive Reframing: Imagine you're wearing a pair of glasses with a gloomy filter. Everything looks bleak and dreary. Now, switch them out for a pair with a rose-tinted filter. Suddenly, the world's a bit brighter. That's cognitive reframing. It's the practice of challenging and changing your perspective on negative situations. When faced with adversity, ask yourself: Is there another way to see this? What can I learn from this situation? What's the silver lining here? By doing this regularly, you'll train your brain to find the positive or, at the very least, the lesson in challenging situations.

2. Journaling: Ah, the art of spilling your thoughts onto paper. It's like giving your mind a good old detox. By jotting down your feelings, you not only vent but also gain clarity on your emotions and triggers. Over time, you might even begin to see patterns, which can be powerful insights for building resilience. After all, understanding your reactions and emotions is half the battle.

3. Mindfulness Practices: Imagine if, instead of getting swept away in a river of emotions, you could simply sit on the bank and watch the water flow by? That's mindfulness. Through practices like meditation, deep breathing, or even mindful walking, you ground yourself in the present moment. This not only reduces stress but also helps you respond to adversity with calm and clarity, rather than react impulsively.

By integrating these practices into your daily life, you're essentially hitting the gym for your resilience muscles. And just like physical training, consistency is key. So, even on the good days, don't skimp on these exercises. Before you know it, you'll be that person who, no matter the setback, always bounces back with gusto.

Picture this: You're at a fancy gala, surrounded by a sea of people donning their finest attire. But instead of feeling like a fish out of water, you stride through, head held high, feeling like you belong, like you're worthy. That sensation, my friend, is self-esteem. It's not about arrogance or thinking you're the bee's knees (although, between us, you totally are). It's about recognizing your value and worth, irrespective of external factors.

Self-esteem is the quiet backbone of our psychological well-being. Think of it as the inner voice that cheers you on when you're facing challenges and gently consoles you during failures. It's the foundation upon which many of our life choices rest. From the relationships we cultivate, the jobs we pursue, to even the hobbies we pick up – it all ties back to how we perceive ourselves.

Now, let's not mince words. The essence of self-esteem is deeply tied to our life satisfaction. When we believe in our worth:

- **We Take Healthy Risks:** Instead of shying away, we lean into challenges because we trust in our abilities and worth.
- **We Set Boundaries:** Knowing our value means we're less likely to tolerate mistreatment or settle for less than we deserve.
- **Our Relationships Flourish:** Because we choose partners who reflect the love and respect we have for ourselves.
- **Stress and Anxiety Diminish:** A strong sense of self-worth acts as a buffer against the uncertainties of life.

On the flip side, a shaky self-esteem can be likened to building a house on sand. No matter how beautiful the exterior, it's vulnerable to even the slightest tremor. This is why investing time and energy in bolstering your self-esteem is not just about feeling good in the moment; it's about setting yourself up for a life filled with contentment, purpose, and joy.

Remember, self-esteem isn't a fixed trait; it's more fluid than you'd think. So, if you're feeling a little low on the self-love scale today, worry not. We're about to delve into some tangible steps to help elevate that inner cheerleader of yours!

The journey to elevating your self-esteem isn't like a sprint; think of it more as a hike. It's about putting one foot in front of the other, enjoying the view, and celebrating every small triumph along the way. And like any hike, you're bound to stumble and face obstacles, but with the right tools in your backpack, you'll reach that summit. So, let's equip you for this adventure!

1. Embrace Positive Self-Talk:

How it works: Our minds are chatterboxes, often buzzing with a commentary on everything we do. If you listen closely, though, you might notice that not all this chatter is kind or constructive. Every time you catch yourself saying, "I can't," or "I'm not good enough," pause. Challenge that thought. Would you talk to a dear friend that way?

Pro-tip: For every negative thought, counter it with three positive affirmations. For example, if you think, "I messed that up," follow it with, "But I've done XYZ well, I learn from my mistakes, and I am capable of improving."

2. Set Achievable Goals:

How it works: Setting monstrous goals can feel overwhelming and can dent your self-esteem when you don't achieve them. Instead, break them down. Start small. Small victories can boost your confidence considerably.

Pro-tip: Use the SMART criteria – Specific, Measurable, Achievable, Relevant, and Time-bound. Instead of saying, "I want to be a better musician," aim for, "I want to practice my guitar for 30 minutes daily for the next month."

3. Celebrate Small Wins:

How it works: Celebrating tiny achievements isn't about being boastful; it's about recognizing the effort you've put in. Did you manage to stick to your new workout routine for a week? That's worth a pat on the back!

Pro-tip: Maintain a 'Win Journal.' Every evening, jot down one or two things you did that day that made you proud. On tough days, flipping through this journal can offer much-needed perspective and a boost.

4. Surround Yourself with Uplifters:

How it works: Just as plants thrive in the right environment, so does your self-esteem. Surrounding yourself with positive, encouraging people can significantly influence how you see yourself.

Pro-tip: Take stock of your social circles. If there's someone consistently dragging you down, it might be time to re-evaluate that relationship.

5. Accept Compliments Graciously:

How it works: When someone praises you, resist the urge to downplay or deflect. They're acknowledging something wonderful about you, and it's okay to agree.

Pro-tip: Practice saying, "Thank you, I appreciate that," without adding a 'but' or brushing the compliment away.

6. Invest in Self-Care:

How it works: Taking time for activities that make you feel good, whether it's reading, taking a bath, or going on a nature walk, sends a strong message to your psyche: "I am worth it."

Pro-tip: Schedule regular self-care dates with yourself, and treat them with the same importance as any other appointment.

Harnessing a sturdy self-esteem isn't about becoming someone new; it's about recognizing and celebrating the incredible person you've been all along. And between you and me? You're pretty darn amazing.

Stepping out from the shadows of past experiences and rebuilding your self-esteem is a significant milestone. But, growth doesn't stop there. Personal growth is a lifelong journey. It's about continuously expanding your horizons, pushing boundaries, and embracing every opportunity for self-improvement. As we dive into this next section, consider it your roadmap to becoming the best version of yourself.

In a rapidly changing world, the ability to adapt is one of the most valuable assets one can have. Here's where the beauty of a growth mindset steps in. Coined by psychologist Carol Dweck, the concept emphasizes the belief that our abilities and intelligence can be developed with effort, training, and perseverance.

Why is this mindset so crucial?

- Fosters Curiosity: When you believe you can learn and grow, every experience becomes a lesson.

Challenges transform from roadblocks into learning opportunities.

- Encourages Resilience: Mistakes aren't setbacks; they're stepping stones. With a growth mindset, you understand that failure is often a precursor to success.
- Drives Innovation: By remaining open to new information and experiences, you become more creative and innovative in your thinking.

How to Cultivate a Growth Mindset:

- Challenge Fixed Beliefs: The next time you think, "I'm just not good at this," reframe it to, "I'm not good at this yet."
- Praise the Process: Instead of just praising results, appreciate the effort, strategy, focus, perseverance, and improvement.
- Stay Curious: Adopt a 'beginner's mind.' Ask questions, seek out new experiences, and continually look for ways to learn.
- Reframe Challenges: Instead of saying, "This is too hard," ask yourself, "What can I learn from this?"

Remember, the brain is like a muscle – the more you challenge it, the stronger it gets. So, keep feeding your curiosity, seek out new experiences, and always be open to learning. The path of continuous learning isn't just about adding skills or knowledge; it's about evolving into a more adaptable, open, and resilient individual.

In the vast expanse of our life's journey, goals serve as the signposts, guiding us towards destinations we aspire to reach. But for these signposts to effectively guide us, they must be clear, actionable, and aligned with our inner values. Enter the world of SMART goals – a framework that ensures our objectives are Specific, Measurable, Achievable, Relevant, and Time-bound.

Why are SMART Goals Important?

1. **Clarity and Direction:** A well-defined goal leaves no room for ambiguity. It offers a clear direction, ensuring you know precisely what to aim for.

2. **Motivation:** Measurable milestones give you the chance to celebrate small achievements, maintaining momentum and enthusiasm throughout your journey.

3. **Focus:** By setting achievable and relevant goals, you concentrate your efforts on what truly matters, eliminating distractions.

4. **Accountability:** With a set timeline, you're more likely to stay committed, regularly assessing your progress and making necessary adjustments.

Creating SMART Goals:

- **Specific (S):** Define your goal as precisely as possible. Instead of "I want to read more," say "I want to read one book per month about personal growth."

- **Measurable (M):** Establish criteria to measure progress. In the above example, the number of books serves as the measure.

- **Achievable (A):** Aim high, but be realistic. If you've never run before, setting a goal to run a marathon next month might be setting yourself up for failure. Instead, start with a 5K.
- **Relevant (R):** Your goals should align with your values and long-term objectives. If health is a core value, a goal around regular exercise or a balanced diet would be fitting.
- **Time-bound (T):** Assign a deadline. Without a timeframe, there's no sense of urgency, making it easy to procrastinate.

Lastly, while the SMART framework offers an effective structure, always leave room for flexibility. Life can be unpredictable, and it's essential to adjust and recalibrate your goals when necessary. Remember, the ultimate aim is personal growth and progress, not rigid adherence to a set plan.

At the core of our actions and reactions lie the beliefs we hold about ourselves, others, and the world around us. Some beliefs propel us forward, igniting our spirit with confidence and enthusiasm. However, others - the limiting beliefs - act as chains, restricting our potential and distorting our self-perception. Often, these beliefs stem from past experiences, societal expectations, or negative feedback. Over time, they weave themselves into the fabric of our psyche, appearing as undeniable truths. The journey to personal growth mandates that we confront these limiting beliefs, challenging their authenticity and reclaiming our narrative.

Recognizing Limiting Beliefs:

1. **Negative Self-talk:** Pay attention to your inner dialogue. Phrases like "I can't," "I'm not good enough," or "Things never go right for me" are red flags.

2. **Fixed Mindset:** If you believe that your qualities and circumstances are static and unchangeable, you likely have some limiting beliefs.

3. **Defensiveness:** When given feedback, do you immediately become defensive, feeling it's an attack on your character or capability?

Strategies to Challenge and Change Limiting Beliefs:

1. **Awareness:** Before changing anything, you must recognize it. Journaling can be a valuable tool. Write down thoughts and beliefs that hold you back, tracing their origins.

2. **Question Their Validity:** Analyze each belief. Is it based on facts or emotions? For instance, just because you failed at a task doesn't mean you're a failure. Separate isolated incidents from global beliefs about your identity.

3. **Replace with Empowering Beliefs:** Once you've identified a limiting belief, intentionally craft an empowering counter-belief. For instance, replace "I can't handle this" with "I will do the best I can."

4. **Evidence Collection:** Seek out evidence that challenges your limiting beliefs. If you believe you're terrible at public speaking, remember times

you've successfully spoken in front of others, even if it was a small group.

5. **Affirmations:** Develop positive affirmations that reinforce empowering beliefs. Repeat them daily, allowing them to seep into your subconscious.

6. **Seek External Feedback:** Sometimes, we're too close to see the bigger picture. Trusted friends, mentors, or therapists can offer insights, helping identify and challenge limiting beliefs.

7. **Educate Yourself:** Read books, attend workshops, or listen to podcasts that delve into personal growth and belief restructuring. Knowledge is power.

8. **Embrace Discomfort:** Changing ingrained beliefs isn't easy. It's uncomfortable. Recognize that discomfort signals growth. Embrace it.

The road to dismantling limiting beliefs isn't linear. It requires patience, effort, and persistence. But as you shed each limiting belief, you'll uncover a more authentic, empowered, and unshackled self, ready to grasp the vast possibilities the world offers. Now that we've seen how to set goals and overcome limiting beliefs, let's see why you need to identify and pursue your passions, and how it can be a source of joy and personal growth.

Passions and pursuits are closely interlinked with our beliefs and aspirations. Just as one needs to set clear objectives in life to navigate the path of self-growth, it's equally pivotal to nurture and chase those inner flames that set our souls alight. While the goals provide direction, our passions infuse the journey with color, vibrancy, and joy. Let's delve deeper into how these personal flames can transform the mundanity of existence into a tapestry of wonder and discovery.

There's a profound beauty in immersing oneself in an activity or pursuit that genuinely lights up the soul. Our passions, those interests and activities that energize and move us, serve as compasses, directing us toward our true north. They aren't just hobbies or pastimes; they are the threads that weave meaning and joy into the fabric of our lives.

In a world brimming with obligations, responsibilities, and an endless barrage of information, it's all too easy to drift away from what makes our hearts sing. And yet, the call of our passions remains, a gentle whisper amidst the cacophony, urging us to remember, to return, to rejoice.

But why is it essential to heed this call? Pursuing passions isn't just about personal pleasure; it's a voyage of self-discovery. When we dive deep into what we love, we unearth facets of ourselves that lay dormant. We tap into reservoirs of creativity, resilience, and determination that we might not have known existed. And in doing so, we sculpt our identities, forming a clearer picture of who we are and what we stand for.

Imagine watching a dancer lost in their routine, every move radiating joy and energy. Or think of the artist, fingers stained with paint, lost in a world of colors and shapes. These individuals aren't just engaging in activities; they're communing with their innermost selves, forging connections that nourish their spirits.

But how does one embark on this journey of passion-pursuit?

Start with Curiosity: Before passion comes curiosity. Allow yourself to explore different avenues without the pressure of mastery. Dabble in activities, attend workshops, or read broadly. Let your curiosity be the guide.

Revisit Your Childhood: Often, our childhood interests and dreams hold clues to our present passions. What activities absorbed you as a child? What dreams did you harbor? Reflecting on these can provide valuable insights.

Commit to the Process: Passion doesn't always equate to immediate excellence. It's okay to be a beginner. It's okay to falter. What's vital is the commitment to keep going, to relish the journey as much as the destination.

Carve Out Time: In our bustling lives, it's crucial to deliberately set aside time for our passions. Whether it's a few minutes daily or a couple of hours weekly, honor this time as sacred, an appointment with your soul.

Share and Connect: Sharing our passions with others can amplify the joy. Whether it's joining a club, attending group classes, or simply sharing your progress with loved ones, let others be a part of your journey.

By identifying and immersing ourselves in our passions, we not only enrich our lives but also contribute uniquely to the world around us. After all, a passionate heart is a radiant heart, shedding light and inspiring everyone in its path.

While chasing our passions and setting goals acts as the fuel and map for our journey of self-growth, it's the people we surround ourselves with that serve as our compass, ensuring we don't lose our way. They offer a hand during stumbles and applaud our triumphs. The significance of this network cannot be overstated. Especially when you've borne the weight of the scapegoat role, these supportive pillars become vital to rebuilding and healing.

Ever recall the sensation of floating, carried forth by invisible wings when someone believed in you during a time of doubt? That's the power of supportive relationships. They're the undercurrents that steer us forward even when our strength wavers. When we've been subjected to years of undue blame and negative labeling, our self-worth can diminish. In these moments, it's the nurturing relationships we forge that act as mirrors, reflecting back our inherent value and strength, reminding us of who we truly are.

For those who have felt marginalized, relationships rooted in mutual understanding, empathy, and respect can be transformative. They don't merely provide a comforting shoulder or a listening ear; they're instrumental in reshaping our perspectives about ourselves. While healing is an inward journey, the path is often lit by those around us who see our potential and beauty even when shadows cloud our self-view.

Embracing and fostering these connections isn't just about seeking solace. It's about laying down bricks for a future where we feel seen, valued, and understood. Because every individual, no matter their past, deserves relationships that celebrate their essence and empower their journey.

In a world bustling with billions, finding your tribe might seem akin to seeking a needle in a haystack. But remember, it's not the number but the nature of connections that truly matter. Your tribe consists of those unique individuals who resonate with your essence, understand your journey, and offer unwavering support. Here's how to embark on the rewarding quest of finding them:

1. Recognize Your Worth: Before seeking your tribe, it's essential to acknowledge your worth. This self-recognition will not only guide you towards people who value you similarly but also ensure you aren't settling for less than what you deserve.

2. Be Authentic: The mask of pretense might win acquaintances but to find a tribe, you must be unabashedly yourself. It's when you showcase your genuine self, with its vulnerabilities and strengths, that you attract individuals who resonate with your core.

3. Attend Interest-Based Groups: Joining clubs, organizations, or groups that align with your passions can be a fruitful way to meet like-minded people. Whether it's a book club, a hiking group, or an art class, shared interests can serve as the foundation for deeper connections.

4. Explore Online Communities: The digital age has been a boon for tribe seekers. Numerous platforms and forums cater to specific interests, experiences, and journeys. Exploring these can help you connect with individuals from around the world who share similar stories or aspirations.

5. Engage in Therapeutic Circles: Therapy isn't just about individual healing. Group therapy sessions or support groups offer an environment where individuals, each grappling with their struggles, come together in a space of mutual understanding and empathy.

6. Stay Open and Patient: Finding your tribe isn't an overnight endeavor. It's a journey. Stay open to meeting diverse individuals, understanding that each person you encounter teaches you something, even if they aren't destined to be a lasting part of your tribe.

Lastly, remember that tribes evolve. As you grow and change, so might your tribe. That's natural and okay. The key is to maintain relationships that empower, uplift, and resonate with your journey at any given point in life.

Healthy relationships form the bedrock of emotional well-being, acting as sanctuaries where we find solace, understanding, and growth. However, establishing and preserving such connections require consistent effort, understanding, and adaptability. Here are some valuable insights to create and nurture these bonds:

Active Listening: True connection stems from genuine understanding, and understanding is cultivated by listening —not just hearing. When conversing, pay full attention to the other person, free from distractions or the urge to frame a response. This active listening allows you to delve into their emotions and perspectives deeply, fortifying the bond of mutual respect.

Open and Honest Communication: Transparent dialogue forms the backbone of any robust relationship. Encourage open-ended discussions where feelings, concerns, and aspirations can be shared without fear of judgment. Remember, it's not just about expressing yourself but also about fostering an environment where the other person feels safe to voice their feelings.

Prioritize Quality Time: In today's digital age, while staying connected is easier, genuine connections are getting rarer. Prioritize spending quality time together, be it through shared activities, deep conversations, or simply being in each other's presence, absorbing the comfort that accompanies it.

Practice Empathy: Put yourself in the other person's shoes. Strive to understand their emotions, reactions, and viewpoints, even if they diverge from yours. This empathetic approach not only helps resolve conflicts more amicably but also deepens the bond of mutual appreciation.

Set and Respect Boundaries: Every individual has their boundaries—be it emotional, physical, or mental. Recognize yours and communicate them clearly, while also understanding and respecting the boundaries set by others. This mutual respect ensures that the relationship flourishes without feelings of being stifled or overstepped.

Celebrate and Support: Be each other's biggest cheerleaders. Celebrate the victories, no matter how big or small, and offer unwavering support during the tougher times. This mutual encouragement strengthens the ties of companionship.

Consistent Effort: Like a garden, relationships bloom when nurtured. Water them with understanding, prune the misunderstandings, and shower them with love and care. This consistent effort ensures that the bond not only remains strong but also grows and adapts over time.

In essence, while every relationship is unique, threaded by its own set of experiences and memories, the principles of mutual respect, understanding, and consistent effort remain

universal. When these principles are cherished and practiced, relationships blossom into sources of unparalleled joy
and comfort.

As much as our personal relationships and self-help strategies can be uplifting, there are moments in life where we
may need a more specialized touch—enter therapy and
counseling. While there's been a progressive decline in the
stigma surrounding mental health support, some still harbor
reservations. Let's shed light on the undeniable benefits of
professional help and guide you on the journey to finding
the right fit.

Benefits of Therapy and Counseling:

Expert Perspective: Therapists provide a neutral,
knowledgeable perspective, allowing for insights that might
be challenging to achieve on your own. Their trained eye
can pinpoint underlying issues and offer tailored strategies
to address them.

Safe Space: A therapy room is a judgment-free zone.
Here, you can bare your soul, discuss your deepest fears,
and cry, rant, or simply talk—all in the assurance of confi-
dentiality and understanding.

Skill Acquisition: Beyond the catharsis of talking,
therapy provides tools and techniques to handle emotional
distress, manage relationships, and navigate life's ups and
downs more effectively.

Enhanced Self-Awareness: Regular sessions often
lead to heightened self-awareness. You become more in
tune with your triggers, your patterns of behavior, and the

whys behind them, empowering you to make informed decisions in your life.

Support in Crisis: During particularly turbulent times, such as trauma or severe anxiety episodes, having a therapist can be a lifeline, providing immediate coping strategies and long-term healing paths.

Finding the Right Professional Help:

Determine Your Needs: Different therapists specialize in different areas—be it trauma, relationships, family therapy, or behavioral disorders. Understanding what you need assistance with can guide your search.

Research and Recommendations: Ask friends or family for recommendations or research online platforms that provide verified therapist listings with reviews.

Check Qualifications: Ensure your chosen therapist is licensed and has the necessary qualifications. Most countries have governing bodies that certify and monitor practicing therapists.

Attend a Few Sessions: Therapy is a deeply personal experience. Sometimes, you might need to meet with a few therapists before you find the one with whom you truly resonate. Remember, it's about the connection as much as the credentials.

Evaluate Costs and Logistics: Therapy can be an investment, both in time and money. Consider the logistics —does the therapist offer sessions that fit your schedule? Do they accept insurance? Are there sliding scale fees available?

Trust Your Gut: Last but not least, trust your intuition. You should feel comfortable, respected, and understood in the presence of your therapist.

In essence, seeking professional support isn't a sign of weakness—it's a testament to your strength and your commitment to self-growth and well-being. Embrace this journey, knowing you're taking a monumental step towards a brighter, healthier future.

In the vast tapestry of life, each individual thread holds a unique story—a journey of highs and lows, moments of despair, and triumphant returns. This chapter is an ode to that resilient spirit within you, the undying flame that refuses to be extinguished, no matter the winds it faces. Resilience is not just about bouncing back; it's about growing from the experience, emerging stronger and more luminous than before.

Through self-esteem, you've rediscovered the art of self-appreciation, of acknowledging your worth, and of refusing to be undervalued. Life's storms may have tried to erode your self-worth, but now, armed with the tools and insights from this chapter, you are ready to rebuild, brick by brick, until you stand tall, filled with the undeniable recognition of your own value.

But this journey, as self-affirming as it is, need not be solitary. There's strength in numbers, in shared experiences, and in mutual understanding. This chapter has illuminated the path to creating a network that uplifts and supports—a tribe that celebrates your victories, offers a shoulder during setbacks, and champions your well-being every step of the way.

In essence, life may have, at times, cast shadows on your path, making you feel confined to a limiting role. But within you lies the power to redefine your narrative, to step into the light, and to radiate your true essence. As you turn the page on this chapter, remember: you are the master of your fate, the captain of your soul. Embrace your inherent worth, take charge of your journey, and watch as the world unfolds in resonance with your reclaimed vibrance.

8

BUILDING AND MAINTAINING HEALTHY RELATIONSHIPS

FROM CHAINS TO CONNECTIONS

There's a profound truth I've come to realize over my years of exploration and introspection: Relationships, in their essence, are the mirrors in which we see reflections of our deepest selves. They can be the vessels of our greatest joys or our most intense sorrows. Imagine, for a moment, being trapped inside a distorted hall of mirrors, each pane reflecting back an exaggerated or minimized version of who you are. That is the daily reality of a family scapegoat, navigating a world where the very relationships that should uplift distort one's image and self-worth. But what if I told you that it's possible to step out of this disorienting maze and into a gallery of true reflections, where relationships become the source of healing, affirmation, and genuine connection? As we delve into this chapter, you'll discover how to transition from the shadows of isolation to the warm embrace of genuine connections, building and maintaining relationships that mirror your true worth.

In a world filled with countless self-help books, podcasts, and Ted talks about love and relationships, it's easy to get lost in the barrage of advice. But if we sift through the myriad opinions, a few universal truths rise to the top. These are the non-negotiables, the foundation stones upon which enduring, nurturing relationships are built. Let's delve into them:

Mutual Respect: At the heart of any thriving relationship is a deep-seated respect for each other. This isn't just about avoiding name-calling during arguments or refraining from belittling comments. It's about seeing the other person as an equal, valuing their opinions, acknowledging their feelings, and treating them with the same kindness and consideration you'd like in return. Remember, respect is the soil from which love grows.

Trust: Imagine building a house on shifting sands; no matter how beautifully you decorate it, without a solid foundation, it's bound to collapse. Trust is that foundation in a relationship. It means believing that the other person has your best interests at heart, even when they're out of sight. It's knowing that they'll keep their promises, be there during the hard times, and remain faithful in both actions and intent.

Open Communication: Have you ever played the game of 'Chinese whispers'? It's amusing in a playful setting but disastrous in a relationship. Clear, open, and honest communication ensures that messages aren't distorted or lost in translation. It's about having the courage to express your feelings, concerns, and dreams, and equally, the patience to listen to your partner's. Communication acts as the bridge between two souls, ensuring that misunderstandings are minimal and connections are genuine.

Emotional Support: Think back to the times you've faced life's storms. Who did you want by your side? Those who'd anchor you or those who'd let you drift away? In a healthy relationship, partners act as each other's anchors. They offer a safe harbor, a comforting embrace, and words of encouragement, ensuring that no challenge feels insurmountable when faced together.

And while these pillars might sound like Relationship 101, it's astonishing how often we compromise on them, especially when our past casts shadows on our present. But recognizing and prioritizing these elements is the first step in ensuring that the love you attract is the kind that heals, uplifts, and endures.

"You know yourself better than anyone else," they say. But how often do we take a pause from our hectic lives to truly introspect? In the realm of relationships, self-awareness is not just a buzzword; it's the compass that helps navigate the complex labyrinth of human connections.

Imagine stepping into a bookstore, overwhelmed by choices, and not knowing what genre you're interested in. It's easy to walk out with a bestseller, only to discover it doesn't resonate with you. Similarly, in the world of relationships, if you aren't aware of what you genuinely want, you may end up with partners who are misaligned with your core values and desires.

1. Understanding Your Needs: Everyone has unique needs in a relationship. Some crave deep emotional intimacy, while others prioritize shared adventures. Knowing where you stand is essential. Are you seeking a partner to share your silence or someone to debate with till dawn?

Recognizing these preferences helps in setting the stage for fulfilling relationships.

2. Reflecting on Past Patterns: Past relationships, including the one with our family, leave indelible marks. Are there recurring patterns you notice? Maybe you tend to attract partners who are emotionally unavailable or those who are overly dominating. Recognizing these patterns can provide insights into subconscious choices you might be making.

3. Establishing Boundaries: A clear sense of self-awareness allows you to establish non-negotiable boundaries. Whether it's about how you'd like to be treated or the amount of personal space you need, understanding these aspects ensures that you aren't swept away in the tide of a relationship, forgetting your essence.

4. Emotional Intelligence: Apart from understanding oneself, self-awareness amplifies emotional intelligence. It allows you to perceive, understand, and manage not just your emotions but also those of your partner. It's the difference between saying, "You're overreacting" and asking, "What's troubling you?"

In essence, self-awareness acts as the North Star. In the vast ocean of relationships, it illuminates the path, ensuring you sail towards shores that resonate with the core of who you are. Because, dear reader, knowing yourself is the first step in finding someone who truly complements you.

But how does one become a magnet for positive, uplifting individuals? As if finding a needle in a haystack isn't challenging enough, we're talking about finding that golden needle that complements your uniqueness. But here's a little secret—it begins with you. Transforming into a beacon for healthy relationships requires an inner shift. Let's navigate this transformative journey together.

1. Cultivate Self-Love:

Before we dive into the nuances, close your eyes for a moment and think of someone you deeply love. How does it feel? That warm, fuzzy feeling? Now, imagine directing that same love towards yourself. Sound strange? It shouldn't.

- **Mirror Talk:** Every morning, gaze into the mirror and offer yourself some words of affirmation. It might feel odd initially, but soon you'll begin to internalize these positive messages.
- **Celebrate Yourself:** Remember to celebrate your victories, big and small. Whether you managed to make a delightful homemade meal or landed a dream job, pat yourself on the back. Celebrating oneself fosters an environment of positivity.

2. Set Boundaries:

Boundaries aren't walls; they're guidelines. They help ensure that interactions and relationships thrive in a healthy ecosystem.

- **Recognize Your Limits:** Understand what you can tolerate emotionally, mentally, and physically. It's essential to know where to draw the line.

- **Communicate Effectively:** Clearly express your boundaries. It's not enough to just know them; others should be made aware too. Remember, it's okay to say 'no.'

3. Prioritize Personal Growth:

Personal growth isn't a destination; it's an ongoing journey. By consistently working on yourself, you inadvertently raise your vibrations, attracting those on a similar wavelength.

- **Never Stop Learning:** Dive into books, attend workshops, or simply engage in thoughtful conversations. Keep the flame of curiosity alive.
- **Embrace Change:** Understand that change is the only constant. Whether it's evolving tastes or shifting beliefs, accept them. It signifies growth.
- **Seek Feedback:** Sometimes, an outsider's perspective can offer invaluable insights. Constructive feedback can be the window to areas you might have overlooked.

Imagine transforming into this radiant sun, emitting warmth, love, and positivity. When you become this beacon, you naturally attract planets—partners who revolve in harmony, complementing your glow. And while the universe might be vast, remember that it often conspires in favor of those who dare to love themselves truly and deeply.

Navigating the labyrinth of human emotions and relationships can sometimes feel like playing detective in your own personal mystery. However, unlike the latest best-selling thriller, this isn't a story you want unexpected plot twists in.

Let's focus on identifying the red flags early on, so you don't end up gasping in surprise down the line.

1. Consistent Lack of Respect:

If your partner belittles you, ignores your feelings, or treats you as inferior, take note. Respect is the cornerstone of any meaningful relationship. Without it, the foundation crumbles.

2. Overwhelming Jealousy:

A smidge of jealousy might be natural, even endearing at times. But when it becomes suffocating, dominating every interaction and decision, it's a glaring red flag.

3. Gaslighting:

If you've ever heard phrases like, "You're overreacting" or "That never happened", be cautious. Gaslighting is a manipulative tactic that makes you question your reality.

4. Constant Criticism:

Constructive feedback is one thing, but if every comment is a jibe or a dig at your self-worth, it's not just a red flag—it's a siren!

5. Isolation from Loved Ones:

If your partner consistently attempts to cut ties between you and your family or friends, it's an alarming sign. Healthy relationships thrive on inclusivity, not isolation.

6. Unequal Power Dynamics:

If decisions are unilaterally made without your input, or if you constantly feel overshadowed, it indicates an imbalance that's detrimental in the long run.

7. Ignoring Boundaries:

Remember the boundaries we just talked about? If they're consistently overstepped or outright ignored, you've got yourself a blatant red flag.

8. Excusing Hurtful Actions as 'Jokes':

If derogatory comments or hurtful actions are brushed off as "just a joke", and especially if they make it seem like you're "too sensitive", beware.

9. Volatility:

Mood swings that oscillate between extreme affection and intense anger create an unpredictable environment and can keep one constantly on edge.

10. Past Patterns:

It's said that the best predictor of future behavior is past behavior. If they've had a history of toxic relationships or have hurt others, proceed with caution.

Recognizing these signs early on can save a world of heartache later. While everyone deserves a chance, and people can change, it's essential to prioritize your mental, emotional, and physical well-being. In the tapestry of relationships, ensure that your thread remains vibrant and unbroken.

With these guidelines in hand, the journey toward healthy relationships becomes clearer and more empowering. Now, let's dive deeper into the intricate dance between healthy and toxic relationship dynamics in the next segment.

As we drift away from the shores of self-awareness and into the vast expanse of relationship dynamics, it's crucial to keep our navigation tools handy. Just as a map guides us through unfamiliar territories, understanding the traits of healthy and toxic relationships ensures we make the right choices in our emotional journeys. Let's set sail with the winds of mutual growth and support, beginning with the hallmarks of healthy relationships.

In the dance of love and partnership, certain melodies harmonize better than others. When the music plays and two people dance in rhythm, a healthy relationship flourishes. These partnerships are more than mere choreography; they're a blend of respect, understanding, and continuous growth.

1. Mutual Respect: At the core of any robust relationship is respect. Both partners value each other's opinions, feelings, and boundaries, ensuring that no one ever feels belittled or dismissed.

2. Open and Honest Communication: A relationship thrives when both parties can express themselves without fear of judgment. They listen actively, making sure their partner feels heard and understood, even during disagreements.

3. Emotional Support: The world can sometimes feel like a stormy sea, but in a healthy relationship, partners serve as each other's anchors. They provide comfort during distressing times, celebrate each other's victories, and offer a shoulder to lean on without conditions.

4. Shared Growth: Both individuals evolve together, recognizing that growth in one person uplifts the other. They're cheerleaders in each other's pursuits, whether personal or mutual.

5. Trust and Reliability: This forms the bedrock of a strong relationship. Partners believe in each other's words and actions, relying on them in times of need, ensuring that vulnerabilities are met with care, not betrayal.

In the realm of love and connection, these elements act as the guiding stars, leading us to the shores of fulfilling and lasting relationships. As we bask in their warmth, it's equally essential to recognize when clouds overshadow this brightness. Let's delve deeper into the opposite end of the spectrum: toxic relationships.

While a healthy relationship feels like a comforting embrace, a toxic one can feel like a tightening grip that leaves you gasping for air. It's that unsettling feeling, like a dissonant note in a harmonious song. These relationships drain more than they replenish, leaving scars that may not always be visible but are profoundly felt.

1. Manipulation: A common tactic in toxic relationships is manipulation. This can manifest in numerous ways, from guilt-tripping to gaslighting. The manipulator aims to control the other person's emotions, decisions, or actions, often making them question their own reality.

2. Constant Criticism: Instead of lifting each other up, if one finds themselves perpetually under the microscope, facing unending scrutiny and negativity, it's a sign of a toxic dynamic. This constant belittlement chips away at self-esteem and self-worth.

3. Unequal Power Distribution: In these relationships, there's an evident power imbalance. One partner may make most decisions, control resources (like finances), or dominate every conversation. The other partner often feels voiceless, as if walking on eggshells.

4. Emotional or Physical Abuse: Perhaps the most alarming sign, abuse can be overt or covert. It ranges from name-calling and shouting to physical violence. Such behavior is never justified and poses significant harm.

5. Jealousy and Possessiveness: A little jealousy is natural, but when it's amplified, it becomes stifling. Overly possessive partners often check phones, control interactions with others, and dictate how their partner should behave, under the guise of "love" or "concern."

6. Lack of Trust: Suspicion lurks in the corners of toxic relationships. Every action is questioned, every word doubted, leading to an environment where partners feel they must defend themselves continually.

7. Neglect and Stonewalling: Emotional neglect, where one's feelings and needs are consistently ignored, can be as damaging as overt abuse. Stonewalling, or giving the silent treatment, is a way of punishing the partner, creating emotional distance.

Understanding these traits is like turning on a flashlight in the dark, revealing the traps and pitfalls on the path. While it's painful to acknowledge such patterns, especially when one has invested emotions, time, and perhaps years into the relationship, knowledge is power. Recognizing these signs offers a chance to reflect, seek help, or make necessary changes. But what about relationships that aren't clearly toxic yet have some of these elements? Let's explore the gray areas next.

Relationships, like the human emotions that fuel them, are seldom black and white. Just as a canvas is not merely made up of stark contrasts but also consists of shades of gray, so too are our interpersonal connections. These 'gray areas' are the spaces where a relationship might not fit the traditional mold of toxicity, yet still brings about unease, doubt, or confusion.

1. Periodic Neglect: Unlike consistent emotional neglect seen in toxic relationships, here, moments of carelessness or oversight come as anomalies rather than the rule. These might be due to external pressures like work stress or health issues but can still cause emotional wounds if not addressed.

2. Passive Aggression: Not as overt as open hostility, passive-aggressive behaviors such as sarcastic remarks, subtle jabs, or the "silent treatment" might make their appearance. While not consistently aggressive, these actions can lead to unresolved feelings and tension.

3. Inconsistent Boundaries: In these relationships, boundaries might fluctuate, leading to confusion. For instance, what was acceptable behavior in one situation might be condemned in another without clear communication.

4. Over-Dependence or Co-dependency: Without reaching the extreme, a relationship might still show signs of unhealthy dependence. Partners might rely heavily on each other for emotional validation, merging their identities in ways that compromise individual growth.

5. Avoidance of Difficult Conversations: Not all conflicts in these gray areas erupt into arguments. Instead, some couples might sidestep important discussions, allowing resentments to simmer under the surface.

6. Fluctuating Dynamics: Power dynamics might not always be imbalanced but could shift from time to time, causing instability. Today's dominant partner might take a backseat tomorrow, leading to unpredictability.

7. Misaligned Values or Goals: Over time, individuals grow, and sometimes that growth can lead to divergent paths. While this isn't toxic per se, if not addressed, it can lead to feelings of disconnection or incompatibility.

Gray areas challenge our perceptions and definitions of what constitutes a "good" or "bad" relationship. They remind us that relationships, like individuals, are complex, evolving entities. Navigating these complexities requires communication, self-reflection, patience, and sometimes, external guidance. It's essential to remember that just because a relationship has gray areas doesn't mean it's doomed. Instead, these moments can be opportunities for growth, understanding, and deepening bonds. However, how does one decide whether to stay and nurture the bond, adjust expectations, or leave? Let's delve into these decision points next.

In the intricate dance of human connections, there often comes a moment when we pause, looking at the face of our partner and wondering, "Is this where I should be?" Such reflection is not an indication of failure, but rather a testament to our innate desire for growth and happiness. Navigating the crossroads of a relationship requires more than just weighing pros and cons. It calls for a deeper introspection into what we desire, value, and deserve.

Tuning Into Your Inner Voice: First and foremost, give yourself permission to truly listen to your feelings. It can be easy to drown our inner voice amidst external pressures, societal norms, or fears of being alone. But authentic happiness stems from aligning with our genuine emotions and needs. Take quiet moments to meditate or journal, allowing your thoughts and feelings to flow without judgment.

Visualizing Your Future: Imagine the trajectory of your relationship five, ten, or even twenty years from now. Does the vision bring warmth, hope, and contentment? Or does it leave you feeling unsettled? Projecting your relationship into the future can provide clarity on whether the current dynamics align with your long-term aspirations.

Open Dialogue: Once you've spent time in introspection, approach your partner with honesty. Expressing your feelings, fears, and hopes can either open doors to mutual growth or provide the closure needed to move in different directions. Remember, it's not about laying blame but seeking understanding.

Seeking Counsel: Sometimes, an external perspective can be invaluable. Whether it's therapy, counseling, or simply confiding in a trusted friend or family member, discussing your relationship concerns can offer fresh insights or reinforce your feelings.

Prioritizing Personal Well-being: The essence of any decision should be your well-being. Relationships should offer comfort, growth, and joy. If you find yourself consistently drained, unhappy, or compromising your values, it may be time to reassess. A relationship shouldn't be the sole source of your happiness but rather an enriching complement to a fulfilling life.

Embracing Change: Life is in perpetual motion. Sometimes, the hardest decision can lead to the most profound growth. Whether you decide to stay and work on your relationship, adjust your expectations, or part ways, embrace the change with the understanding that every experience contributes to your journey of self-discovery and happiness.

In conclusion, relationships are dynamic, reflecting the ever-evolving nature of human beings. Decisions regarding them are deeply personal and unique to every individual and situation. At every crossroad, let love for yourself be your compass, guiding you toward genuine happiness and fulfillment.

Transitioning from the broader dynamics of relationships, let us delve into a more personal narrative, illuminating the path from shadowed isolation to the warmth of genuine connection.

Growing up as the designated family scapegoat is akin to living in a beautiful garden but being confined within a dark, lonely corner. The vibrant colors, laughter, and joy seemed almost touchable, but an invisible barrier constantly kept them out of reach.

In this family, my role was clear. I was the mirror reflecting everything that went wrong, absorbing the frustrations, the disappointments, and the angers. Every mishap was somehow connected to me, every discord somehow my doing. The weight of blame was an ever-present shadow, shaping my reality, muddling my self-worth, and embedding a nagging feeling of inadequacy.

Social gatherings and family dinners were the hardest. Surrounded by voices, laughter, and sometimes even love, an insurmountable wall of isolation shielded me. It seemed as though I was on the outside looking in, yearning to belong but constantly reminded of my "assigned place."

One summer evening, I found myself at a local park, watching families enjoy picnics, children laughing, and couples sharing whispered secrets. It was a scene of connection, a stark contrast to the loneliness I felt. But amidst the crowd, an elderly woman sat alone, her eyes deep with wisdom and understanding. Drawn to her, I initiated a conversation, which flowed into stories of her life, her regrets, and her joys.

It was her words that sparked a flame within me. She said, "Sometimes, the families we're born into are just the starting chapters of our stories. The rest is up to us to write." It dawned on me that waiting for acceptance from my family might never bring the connection I yearned for. I needed to seek it outside, to create my own narrative, to define my worth.

Emboldened by that realization, the quest began. I enrolled in community classes, joined interest groups, volunteered at shelters, and most importantly, sought therapy to untangle the web of self-doubt and internalized blame. Each step was a challenge. Trust didn't come easily, and the fear of rejection often loomed large. There were moments of setbacks, days when old wounds felt fresh, and nights when loneliness felt like a familiar companion.

Yet, with time, genuine connections formed. Some relationships blossomed quickly, while others took their sweet time.

But every shared laughter, every comforting hug, and every understanding glance chipped away at the walls of isolation.

From this journey emerged insights that became the cornerstones of my life. I learned that self-worth isn't a reflection of external blame or praise but an intrinsic value we all possess. Genuine connections aren't based on familial ties but on mutual respect, understanding, and love. But perhaps the most pivotal realization was that it's never too late to rewrite one's narrative. From the shadows of being a scapegoat, I found the light in connections that celebrated authenticity, vulnerability, and growth.

In the end, life's essence lies not in how we begin our story, but in how we choose to continue it. The transformative power of genuine connections is a testament to our innate ability to evolve, heal, and thrive.

Our relationships shape our narratives, influence our emotions, and ultimately determine the quality of our lives. Through this chapter, we've navigated the multifaceted nature of human connections, from the foundational pillars of healthy relationships to the murkier terrains of toxicity.

Yet, above all, the resonating message is clear: Relationships are more than mere affiliations; they are the vessels through which we experience life's highs and lows. Prioritizing our well-being in these relationships is not just a right but an inherent duty to ourselves. By doing so, we not only elevate our own experiences but also contribute positively to the lives of those around us.

But perhaps the most transformative lesson is understanding our innate worthiness of love and connection. No matter your past, the roles you've been thrust into, or the shadows you've battled, you deserve relationships that nurture, uplift, and resonate with the core of who you are. The journey towards genuine connection may be rife with challenges, but the destination, a life enriched with deep bonds, is worth every step.

As we close this chapter, may you be empowered with the knowledge and insights shared. May you recognize the dynamics that serve you and those that don't. And most importantly, may you be continually inspired to seek, build, and cherish relationships that mirror the boundless love and connection you inherently deserve.

9

MOVING FORWARD

NEW HORIZONS, TRUE IDENTITY

Like the Phoenix, symbolizing rebirth and renewal in its majestic flight from the ashes, every individual possesses the incredible power to shed the weight of past roles, emerging renewed and empowered. The path we've walked thus far in this book has been one of discovery, reflection, and transformative healing. In this chapter, we delve deep into the next phase of this odyssey - the art of moving forward, of asserting your newfound identity with grace and unshakeable confidence. The chains that once bound you in the role of the family scapegoat are broken, and you stand at the precipice of a new dawn. But as with any rebirth, this phase brings its own challenges, nuances, and invaluable lessons. Let's embrace this journey, understanding that with every step we take, we're not just moving forward, but soaring upwards, much like the Phoenix, into a sky of boundless possibilities.

> You are not who you think you are. Rather, you are who you think.

This phrase, though deceptively simple, is rooted in the profound psychological principle that our perception of ourselves largely influences the course of our lives. Our self-perception, the internal dialogue and image we hold about ourselves, acts as the director's lens through which we view and interact with the world around us.

Consider for a moment the role of the family scapegoat. If you've internalized this identity, you might find yourself habitually occupying spaces of blame, shouldering burdens that aren't yours, or constantly seeking validation. Over time, these behaviors aren't just reactions to external situations but become deeply ingrained patterns, influencing decisions, relationships, and even career paths.

Similarly, if you perceive yourself as incapable or unworthy, you might shy away from opportunities, avoid healthy risks, or settle for less in relationships and professional pursuits. On the flip side, a self-perception grounded in self-worth, confidence, and optimism can propel you to pursue your dreams, establish fulfilling relationships, and craft a life trajectory marked by growth, joy, and resilience.

It's crucial to understand this potent connection between how we view ourselves and the life we manifest. For in recognizing this link, we're handed the reins of control, enabling us to consciously reshape our narrative, redefine our identity, and redirect the course of our destiny.

Creating a new identity, particularly when shedding deeply entrenched roles, is akin to sculpting – it requires patience, dedication, and a clear vision. While the journey is deeply personal, a general roadmap can guide your transformative odyssey:

Reflection:

- **Understanding the Past:** Begin by delving into your past. Understand the moments, interactions, and influences that shaped your former identity. Ask yourself: How did I become the family scapegoat? What patterns emerged from that role? Journaling can be a powerful tool in this phase, helping you map out your feelings, memories, and realizations.

- **Identifying Limiting Beliefs:** Recognize beliefs and internal dialogues that held you back. Statements like "I always mess up" or "No one values my opinion" are self-defeating scripts that need rewriting.

- **Acknowledging Strengths:** Your past identity doesn't define your entirety. Amidst the struggles, you've undoubtedly exhibited strengths and achieved successes. Recognize them. They're the building blocks for your new identity.

Envisioning:

- **Dream Without Boundaries:** Imagine the version of yourself you aspire to become. What values do they uphold? How do they interact with others? What are their passions and dreams?

- **Visualize Success:** Engage in guided visualizations or meditations. Imagine yourself confidently asserting boundaries, pursuing passions, or simply enjoying life without the shadow of past roles.

- **Craft a Personal Mission Statement:** This will serve as your North Star, guiding your actions and decisions in alignment with your envisioned identity.

Active Role-Playing:

- **Take Baby Steps:** Start by consciously adopting one attribute or behavior of your new identity. It could be as simple as voicing an opinion during a family discussion or taking up a new hobby.
- **Challenge Yourself:** Place yourself in situations where you can actively practice this new identity. For instance, if you envision yourself as more assertive, practice assertiveness in safe environments, like a discussion group.
- **Seek Feedback:** Discuss your transformation journey with close friends or mentors. They can provide valuable feedback, helping you fine-tune your behaviors and align them with your envisioned identity.

As you embark on this process, remember that reimagining oneself isn't about becoming someone else, but rather, it's about fully realizing and embracing who you inherently are, minus the layers of imposed roles and expectations. It's a journey to your most authentic self.

Often, in our pursuit of transformation, we get so focused on the destination that we neglect the journey's value. However, true growth, particularly when reinventing one's identity, is an accumulation of countless moments, choices, and, yes, even setbacks. It's in these moments that the seeds of transformation are sown and watered. Therefore, the celebration of small wins isn't just a feel-good activity; it's a crucial part of the entire reinvention process.

Let me break it down for you:

Affirmation of Progress: By celebrating minor achievements, you're acknowledging that you're moving forward. It might not be a giant leap, but hey, even baby steps take you closer to your destination. Think of it as giving yourself a pat on the back, whispering, "I'm proud of you, keep going."

Building Momentum: Celebrating creates a positive feedback loop. The joy and pride you feel when acknowledging a win, no matter how small, fuels your motivation. This momentum is incredibly valuable, propelling you towards your next achievement with renewed vigor.

Shifting Perspective: When you focus on what you've achieved, instead of solely what's left to achieve, it shifts your perspective from scarcity to abundance. This shift fosters a mindset of gratitude and optimism.

Reinforcement of Desired Behaviors: Neuroscience has shown that when you reward a behavior, even if it's just with self-praise or a treat, you're reinforcing it. Over time, these reinforced behaviors become ingrained, gradually molding your new identity.

Resilience in the Face of Setbacks: Let's be real; the journey isn't always smooth. There will be bumps and detours. Celebrating small wins serves as a reservoir of positivity, enabling you to bounce back from setbacks with resilience.

In essence, celebrating small wins is like dotting the i's and crossing the t's in the story of your transformation. Each dot and cross, though minute, is integral to the narrative. So, go ahead, take a moment, maybe even right now, to acknowledge something you've achieved recently. Give yourself the credit you rightfully deserve. It's not just about the destination, dear reader; it's also about savoring every step along the way.

As we navigate the waters of personal transformation, it's essential to acknowledge the ripples our changes create in the world around us. External feedback, whether from friends, family, or even strangers, can serve as a guiding compass, affirming our direction or suggesting course corrections. This feedback, especially when positive, can be a beacon, highlighting our progress and bolstering our resolve. So, let's dive into understanding the profound influence of positive reinforcement from our environment and how it can solidify our emerging identity.

Let's start with a little experiment. Remember a time when someone complimented your new haircut, outfit, or perhaps a skill you showcased? Now, recall how that made you feel. There's a good chance you stood a little taller, smiled a little wider, and felt a spring in your step. This simple example serves to illustrate the profound impact external feedback can have on us. Now, let's delve into its role in shaping and solidifying a new identity.

Mirror to Our Progress: At times, we might be our own harshest critics. This is especially true during periods of transition or self-improvement. Positive feedback from our peers acts as an external mirror, reflecting our progress, which we might overlook. When someone notices and acknowledges a change in you, it's like getting a tangible marker of your journey.

Boosts Self-Confidence: There's a certain magic in external validation. While the journey of reinvention is deeply personal and should be internally driven, there's no denying that positive reinforcement boosts our self-confidence. It's like getting a nudge and whisper, "You're on the right path, keep going."

Reinforces the New Identity: When people around you begin to recognize and treat you in line with your new identity, it reinforces your perception of this identity. Over time, this continual reinforcement helps in making this new identity feel more 'you' and less like a role you're trying on.

Encourages Consistency: Positive reinforcement can also act as a motivator. When our efforts are recognized and praised, we're more likely to stay consistent in our behaviors and actions that align with our new identity. Think of it as a societal "thumbs up" guiding you forward.

The Cautionary Note: While positive external feedback is a powerful tool, it's essential to remember not to become solely reliant on it. Your journey of reinvention should be rooted in self-belief and internal validation. External feedback is the cherry on top, not the entire sundae.

In essence, while carving out a new identity, the external world acts as a feedback loop, continually reflecting, reinforcing, and sometimes refining our inner transformation. It's the dance between our internal desires and external affirmations that truly solidifies change. So, the next time someone acknowledges the 'new you', take a moment to bask in it, thank them, and remember - every piece of positive reinforcement is another brick in the monument of your new identity. Just ensure that your foundation is always built on self-awareness and self-worth.

Change is an incredibly powerful force, but like a river's current, it has its ebbs and flows. Sometimes, as we move forward in our personal growth, unseen forces pull us back to our old ways, making us feel as if we've been swept back to square one. However, understanding these forces is our best defense against them. The first step in safeguarding our newfound identity is to recognize the triggers that threaten to plunge us back into the familiar role of the scapegoat.

Certain situations, people, or emotions can act as anchors, dragging us back into a sea of past memories and behaviors. These triggers could be an offhand comment from a relative, a particular family gathering, or even a specific song or scent that brings back old feelings. Recognizing these triggers is pivotal, as being aware allows us to brace ourselves and respond proactively, rather than reactively, ensuring our growth remains on course.

When a gust of wind topples a tree, it's not just the force of the wind but the tree's rigidity that causes it to fall. In our journey of transformation, flexibility and resilience are our allies, especially when faced with triggers that threaten to revert us to our old roles. It's not about avoiding these triggers but developing coping strategies to navigate through them. Here's how you can stand tall and firm, like the deeply rooted oak, even in the stormiest of situations:

Deep Breathing: It might sound cliché, but the act of taking deep, purposeful breaths does wonders. Whenever you feel a rush of emotions, pause and take three deep breaths. This simple act can give your mind the momentary break it needs to process the situation and react with composure.

Journaling: Sometimes, our minds become a whirlwind of thoughts, making it difficult to think clearly. In such moments, grab a pen and paper. Write down your feelings, the situation, and why it affected you so profoundly. Over time, this exercise not only provides clarity but can also reveal patterns in your triggers, empowering you to handle them better.

Seek Support: Remember, it's okay to lean on others. Whether it's a close friend, a support group, or a therapist, talking it out can provide a fresh perspective. Their external viewpoint can often shed light on aspects you might have overlooked. Moreover, just the act of sharing and feeling understood can be incredibly healing.

Mindfulness and Meditation: Practicing mindfulness helps you stay in the present moment. Instead of being swept away by emotions, you can observe them from a distance, understanding them without becoming them. Daily meditation, even if it's just for a few minutes, strengthens this skill.

Affirmations: Create a list of positive affirmations that resonate with your new identity. Whenever you feel a trigger trying to pull you back, recite these affirmations either mentally or aloud. It's like a shield, reinforcing your new self-beliefs.

Time-out Technique: If a situation gets too overwhelming, give yourself permission to step away. A short walk, a few minutes of solitude, or even immersing yourself in a different activity can act as a reset button.

By integrating these techniques into your daily life, you're not just countering triggers; you're fortifying your new identity against any challenge that comes its way. Remember, it's not about never facing challenges but having the tools to navigate through them.

In the mosaic of life, each individual is a unique piece, contributing to the larger picture. Just as two pieces must fit well without overshadowing each other, boundaries in relationships, especially familial ones, ensure a harmonious coexistence. But when it comes to families that have deep-seated dynamics, establishing and maintaining boundaries can be both crucial and challenging.

Family is a powerful force in our lives. The bonds, the shared history, and the profound influences shape much of who we are. Yet, it's in this very space of love and comfort that we sometimes find our boundaries most tested. Old roles, like that of the scapegoat, aren't just individual labels but a part of the larger family narrative. When one member starts changing their part, it can unsettle the entire story.

Think of it like a well-rehearsed play. If one actor suddenly changes their lines, it confounds the rest. The family, in many ways, is like this play, and when the scapegoat begins to speak a new language of self-worth and assertiveness, it's unfamiliar and even threatening to the established dynamics.

Maintaining boundaries, particularly with those who might unconsciously pull you back, is a delicate dance of love and assertiveness. Here's why it's indispensable:

Personal Growth: Every individual has the right to evolve, grow, and find their path. By setting boundaries, you're carving out the space you need for personal development without the weight of old roles holding you back.

Emotional Health: Consistently being pulled into a role that no longer aligns with your self-perception can be draining. Boundaries protect your emotional well-being, allowing you to engage with family on your terms.

Transforming Dynamics: By establishing and maintaining boundaries, you're not just protecting yourself but also gently guiding your family towards a healthier, more supportive dynamic. It paves the way for others to introspect and perhaps reevaluate their roles as well.

Self-respect: Every time you uphold a boundary, you send a message – not just to others but to yourself – that you value your peace, growth, and happiness.

However, it's essential to remember that setting boundaries is not about building walls but creating respectful spaces for individuality within the family fabric. It's a journey of patience, understanding, and consistent effort, but the rewards — a more authentic relationship with oneself and one's family — are truly invaluable.

Amid the ever-changing landscapes of our lives, one constant remains: the innate human desire to grow, evolve, and flourish. Every sunrise offers a fresh canvas, a new beginning to paint our dreams, learn from our past, and reach for what lies just beyond the horizon. Life's true adventure isn't in the destinations we reach but in the transformation we undergo along the way.

Imagine a seed, ensconced in the dark earth, its potential unseen. With time, nurturing, and an unwavering spirit, it breaks through the soil, reaching for the sunlight. This journey from a dormant seed to a blooming plant is laden with challenges — harsh weather, scarce resources, and the ever-present pull of the ground beneath. Yet, the seed never ceases its growth. It knows that its true essence is not to remain buried but to blossom. We are not much different from this seed. Within each of us lies the potential to transcend our limitations, face our challenges head-on, and blossom into the best versions of ourselves.

Staying committed to personal development is more than just a pursuit; it's a declaration to oneself and the world. It's an acknowledgment that while our past has shaped us, it doesn't confine us. Our journey of growth is an ever-winding path, laden with both revelations and setbacks. But every step, every stumble, and every stride forward refines us.

Here are some inspirations to keep in mind:

Embrace the Journey: Recognize that personal growth is not a destination but a continuous journey. There will be peaks and valleys, but each phase offers its lessons. Cherish them.

Seek Inspiration: Surround yourself with people, stories, and experiences that inspire and challenge you. Let the world be your teacher.

Be Kind to Yourself: On this path, remember to be your own biggest supporter. Celebrate your victories, however small, and learn from your setbacks without self-judgment.

Stay Curious: Keep the flame of curiosity alive. Seek new experiences, ask questions, and always remain open to learning.

Trust the Process: Even when the path seems uncertain, trust in your journey and your potential. Sometimes growth is silent and unseen, but it's always at work.

In this grand tapestry of existence, every individual thread, with its twists and turns, contributes to the beauty of the whole. As you weave your story, remember that every moment of growth, every insight, and every challenge surmounted not only elevates you but also adds to the world's richness.

So, as you stand at the crossroads of the familiar and the unknown, dare to dream, dare to evolve, and most importantly, dare to grow. For in growth, we find our purpose, our joy, and our true essence.

As we journey through our own tales of transformation, sometimes the most profound insights come not from textbooks or experts, but from personal experiences that deeply resonate with our souls. I'd like to share one such pivotal moment in my life, a moment that crystallized the complexities and emotions of my journey to shed the scapegoat role and embrace my true self.

The Days Before: A Whirlwind of Anticipation

Days seemed to transform into mere fleeting moments as the date of the family reunion approached. Each ticking second of the clock brought with it a cascade of emotions, a mix of excitement and anxiety, hope and trepidation. For years, family gatherings had been a backdrop for my assigned role, the one where I was the 'easy target,' the perennial scapegoat for collective frustrations and unresolved issues.

Memories of past reunions played like a familiar movie in my mind. The subtle jabs, the not-so-subtle comments, and that ever-pervading sense of being the 'odd one out.' Each memory was punctuated with an accompanying emotion: the sting of humiliation, the weight of disappointment, and the heat of silent anger. But this reunion was different, or at least, I wanted it to be. It was the first since I had embarked on my transformative journey.

Mixed in with the apprehension were pockets of hope. I had grown, evolved, and found my voice. The idea of showcasing this newfound self to the very group that had, perhaps inadvertently, contributed to my earlier self-doubt was both thrilling and terrifying. Would they see the change? Would they embrace it? Or would old patterns resurface, pulling me back into the abyss of my past role?

The eve of the reunion, I stood before my reflection, searching the eyes staring back for a sign of the strength I had cultivated. I had armed myself with knowledge, self-awareness, and coping mechanisms. But was I ready? Only time would tell.

The Day of Revelation: Navigating the Familiar Terrain with New Eyes

The soft chime of the doorbell signaled the beginning of the reunion. The familiar sounds of laughter and chatter soon filled the air, enveloping the room in a cocoon of nostalgia. Family members exchanged hugs, recounted tales of yester-years, and updated each other on recent happenings. From a corner, I observed, taking a moment to breathe and ground myself before diving into the whirlpool of interactions.

Aunt Martha, always the life of the party, was the first to approach me. With her boisterous laugh and large gestures, she exclaimed, "Look at you! All grown-up and serious! Remember when you'd always spill the punch at these gath-erings?" A memory I had hoped to forget. While the comment was made in jest, the undertones of the past were evident. But instead of retreating into the shadows of humil-iation, I smiled, choosing to reply playfully, "Well, Aunt Martha, some things never change. But I've traded the punch for coffee now."

As the evening progressed, various family members approached, some with genuine curiosity about my life and others with veiled remarks, testing the waters of my trans-formation. My cousin Jake, with whom I shared a competi-tive yet supportive bond, remarked, "Heard you're doing well at your job. Must feel good to finally get something right." A comment that would have previously evoked defensiveness or shame instead prompted a calm response. "Thanks, Jake. Every step is a learning experience, and I'm enjoying the journey."

Internally, each interaction was a test of resilience. There were moments when the weight of the past threatened to overshadow the present. The familiar pangs of anxiety, the quickened heartbeat, the flush of embarrassment – they all made fleeting appearances. But with each encounter, I reminded myself of the growth I had achieved, the battles I had conquered, and the self-worth I had painstakingly built.

However, not all interactions were fraught with tension. Many family members genuinely celebrated my achievements and growth. Grandma, with her infinite wisdom and ever-supportive demeanor, whispered in my ear, "I always knew you had it in you. Proud of the person you're becoming." Such moments of genuine connection and recognition served as fuel, pushing me forward, reminding me of the validity of my journey.

As the night wore on, I realized that while the setting and characters remained familiar, the script had changed. I was no longer the silent recipient of misplaced frustrations or the butt of every joke. Instead, I was an active participant in the narrative, choosing my responses, setting boundaries, and, most importantly, honoring my journey and growth.

A Dance Between Old Shadows and New Light

The family reunion was not merely a gathering of kin; it became a vivid tapestry of moments, both uplifting and challenging, as I navigated the dynamics with my renewed sense of self.

One of the most triumphant moments came during a group conversation about careers. Uncle Robert, ever the critic, posed a question, thinly veiled with skepticism, about the stability of my current job. Instead of faltering, I confidently shared my achievements, drawing attention to the passion and dedication I put into my work. The approving nods and genuine interest from other family members felt like a soft glow of validation. It was a moment where I stood tall in my new identity, showcasing my growth without the shadow of doubt.

Another highlight was when younger cousin Lily approached me, seeking advice on handling bullying at school. In the past, I might've shied away, haunted by my own memories. But now, I embraced the opportunity to guide her, leveraging my experiences not as painful memories but as lessons to empower another. It was a testament to the transformative power of perspective.

However, the evening wasn't devoid of challenges. As the family shared memories, some took trips down lanes that were better left untraveled. A particular jest about a childhood mishap, told with exaggerated flair by Cousin Derek, stirred the old feelings of embarrassment. For a brief moment, I felt like that awkward child again, out of place and seeking approval. It was a stark reminder of the vulnerabilities that still lay beneath the surface.

Dinner brought another test. Seated beside Aunt Clara, the conversation inevitably drifted towards past family dramas. Her words, dripping with nostalgia for days gone by, threatened to drag me back into the scapegoat role. The internal tug-of-war was palpable - a part of me yearning to correct her misconceptions, while another urged retreat into familiar, passive silence. It was in this moment of struggle that I chose a middle path, acknowledging her memories but gently steering the conversation towards neutral grounds.

The dance of the evening was intricate, a delicate balance between showcasing the empowered self I had become and confronting the shadows of a past role I no longer wished to play. Every interaction was a step in the dance, sometimes forward in triumph and at other times, a slight stumble into doubt. But through it all, the rhythm of growth and self-awareness played the guiding tune.

Embracing the Continuum of Growth

The family reunion, while a single event in the timeline of my life, became an emblematic reflection of the broader journey I had embarked upon. It was a microcosm, teeming with the complexities of familial ties, past narratives, and the undying quest for self-realization.

To many, reunions are a mirror to the past, a nostalgic revisit to bygone days. However, for me, this gathering was not just a backward glance but also a litmus test for the strides I had made in my personal evolution. While the past sought to tether me with its familiar strings, my new identity constantly urged me to break free, to redefine the stories told and to reshape the interactions unfolding.

The significance of this reunion was not in its capacity to drag me back into old roles but in the revelations it offered. It underscored the reality that growth is non-linear. There are moments of soaring and instances of faltering. But each interaction, each memory revisited, and each emotion felt added a layer to the mosaic of my transformation.

Beyond the scapegoat role, I realized the journey isn't about completely erasing old scars or about rewriting history. It's about embracing the entirety of one's experiences, drawing strength from vulnerabilities, and crafting a narrative that reflects not just the struggles, but more importantly, the triumphs and the relentless spirit of progress. As I departed the reunion, I left with more than just memories; I carried with me a reinforced conviction in my journey, an affirmation of my new identity, and the invaluable lesson that the dance of growth, with its highs and lows, is an enduring one.

The chapters of our lives are written not just by fate, but also by the ink of our choices, reflections, and aspirations. The voyage from being pigeonholed as the scapegoat to embracing a more authentic and empowered self is arduous yet incredibly enriching. It's a testament to the human spirit's resilience and its boundless capacity for reinvention.

The journey doesn't conclude with the mere shedding of old roles. It's an ongoing dance of self-awareness, growth, and evolution, with each step deepening our understanding of who we are and what we can become. At times, the pull of the past might seem overwhelmingly strong, tempting us to regress to familiar yet limiting roles. Yet, it's essential to remember that with every challenge surmounted, with every negative narrative countered, we weave yet another resilient thread into the tapestry of our identity.

You have within you an innate power, an indomitable spirit that can shape destiny, write new narratives, and redefine legacy. As you step into each day, be reminded of this strength. Treasure the small triumphs, learn from the setbacks, and continuously nurture the newly formed perceptions of self. In this odyssey of self-discovery and redefinition, stay rooted in your truth, for it is there, in the heart of authenticity, that you'll find the compass guiding you to your destined shores.

CONCLUSION
THE ODYSSEY OF OVERCOMING

As we stand on the precipice of closing this enlightening chapter of our journey together, it's vital to take a moment to reflect. Together, we have traversed the labyrinthine corridors of family dynamics, delved deep into the heartaches and triumphs, and emerged on the other side with a newfound understanding. It has been no easy task. The layers we've peeled back, the stories we've shared, and the raw emotions we've grappled with speak to the profound roller coaster that understanding and transcending the scapegoat role has been.

It's no small feat to delve deep into the recesses of past traumas, to face them head-on, and to seek a path beyond them. In many ways, this book has been an expedition—a journey into the heart of the family structure, its pitfalls, and its redemptive arcs. You, dear reader, have shown incredible resilience, courage, and introspection as you've navigated each page, each revelation. The layers of your self-awareness, the tapestry of your experiences, and the intricate web of your emotions have all been honored and celebrated here.

I, too, have been on this ride, sharing my personal anecdotes and insights, reliving some of my most challenging moments, and, in the process, hopefully, illuminating a path for you. The tales from my past were not always easy to share, but they were necessary. They serve as testament to the adage that we truly can rise from our histories, no matter how confining or challenging they may have been.

The landscape of the scapegoat role in family dynamics is fraught with challenges. However, just as the valleys give depth to the mountains, so too do the lows of our experiences offer contrast to our highs. Our shared journey through these pages has been about finding those peaks, elevating ourselves, and stepping into the sunlight of understanding and growth.

As we journeyed through the chapters, several pivotal insights came to the fore. We began by unraveling the dynamics surrounding the family scapegoat, tracing its roots through historical and cultural contexts and understanding the intricate reasons one might be cast in this role. The emotional toll of being the scapegoat was laid bare, exposing the deep-seated feelings and long-term psychological impacts. Recognizing the patterns became the beacon of light, a guide to discerning the signs and interactions that perpetuate the scapegoat cycle. Yet, knowledge alone isn't power; applying it is. We delved into the tangible steps to break this cycle, emphasizing boundaries and transformative family engagements. Healing the wounds was paramount, as was the importance of self-care and self-love in the recuperation process. We then charted the course to reclaim life and personal power, understanding the essence of resilience, and the strength derived from a supportive network. Our exploration on building and maintaining healthy relationships laid the foundation for a future free from the shadows of past roles. Finally, as we envisioned a life beyond the scapegoat label, the focus shifted to fostering a new identity and warding off relapses into old patterns.

However, amidst these layers of insights and strategies, there's a transformative power in the simple act of recognition. Realizing one's role as the family scapegoat can be the pivotal turning point in the journey of healing and self-discovery. This acknowledgment is akin to turning on a light in a long-darkened room, revealing corners and spaces previously unknown. Once you see, you cannot unsee; and with that recognition, the seeds of change are sown. The weight of the role, the burden of unjust blame, starts to lift the moment you name it and claim your right to move beyond it. The journey from this initial spark of awareness to full-blown transformation may be long, but it begins with that single, powerful step of recognition.

Embarking on this transformative journey is no small feat, and it's essential to pause and applaud yourself for the tremendous progress you've made. Whether you've just begun to recognize the patterns or have taken significant strides in breaking free, each step signals a personal triumph. Some days, merely getting up and choosing hope over despair is a monumental victory. Every realization, every boundary set, every tear shed in understanding and every moment of self-love is a testament to your resilience and strength. Remember, healing isn't a linear path. There will be peaks and troughs, moments of clarity, and bouts of doubt. But every step, no matter how tiny, propels you forward, away from the shadows of the scapegoat role and into the light of self-worth and empowerment.

The journey toward healing, while deeply personal, doesn't demand solitude. There's immense power in seeking and accepting support, be it from friends, therapists, or support groups. Recognize that you're not alone in your struggles, nor do you have to bear the weight of healing by yourself. Building and nurturing a supportive network can make the path less daunting, offering encouragement during the lows and celebrating the highs. Surrounding yourself with under-standing and compassionate individuals can make all the difference, transforming the journey from a solitary hike to a communal pilgrimage, each member uplifting the other. Remember, there's strength in numbers, and together, you can rise above the past, forging a brighter, shared future.

The shadows of our past, no matter how long or dark, cannot overshadow the radiant potential of our future. It's true that the roles we were cast into, the labels slapped onto us, have shaped parts of who we are. But they don't define us in totality. Every sunrise brings with it a new beginning, a fresh page waiting to be written upon. Your history, while significant, is but one chapter of an epic tale that's still unfolding. By confronting and understanding the past, you've taken the power to pen the next chapters, carving a narrative that resonates with your dreams, desires, and true self. Think of it as rewriting a story where the protagonist, after facing numerous trials, finally emerges stronger, wiser, and with a heart full of hope.

Imagine a horizon painted with endless possibilities, where every day is an opportunity to discover, grow, and revel in the joy of being authentically you. A future where the chains of the scapegoat role are left far behind, and in its place, there's an unburdened soul dancing to the rhythms of freedom. This isn't a mere daydream; it's a tangible reality that awaits. As you continue on this path, you'll find pockets of happiness in unexpected places, build meaningful connections based on mutual respect, and bask in the warm glow of self-worth. This future is devoid of labels, brimming instead with laughter, love, and countless moments of genuine connection.

Every individual, including you, is a mosaic of experiences, dreams, strengths, and vulnerabilities. At the core of this complex being lies an undeniable truth - an innate worthi-ness of love, respect, and understanding. This belief isn't conditional on past roles or societal labels; it's a birthright. Embracing self-worth is like igniting a flame within, a flame that can dispel the darkest doubts and fears. As you begin to recognize and cherish your intrinsic value, you'll find that the world, in reflection, starts treating you with the same love and respect. It all begins with looking in the mirror and understanding that the person staring back, flaws and all, is profoundly worthy of all the love in the world.

Your journey, intricate and deeply personal, has only just begun. With each day, there's a new chapter to be written, a new lesson to be learned, and a new horizon to explore. It's tempting, sometimes, to think that reaching a certain mile-stone means the journey's end. But self-discovery, like the meandering rivers, doesn't have a fixed destination; it's an ongoing expedition filled with rapids and serene stretches alike. So, as you move forward, wear your scars with pride, cherish the insights you gather, and always remain a student of life. After all, every sunrise offers a fresh canvas, and the artist within you holds the brush.

If your journey has taught you anything, it's the transformative power of shared experiences. Your story, with its highs and lows, has the potential to be a beacon of hope for someone else navigating the stormy seas of self-doubt and societal labels. By sharing your tale, your struggles, and your triumphs, you not only validate your experiences but also illuminate the path for others. Think of it as passing the torch in a relay where every story shared adds more light, dispelling the engulfing darkness bit by bit.

Every story has magic within, an alchemy that transforms pain into purpose, tears into triumphs. Your journey, with its unique blend of challenges and victories, holds within it the power to inspire, to heal, and to create ripples of change. Never underestimate the strength of your narrative. For someone out there, hearing your tale might just be the turning point they've been waiting for, the sign that they too can overcome, heal, and flourish. So, hold your story close to your heart, but let its echoes reach far and wide, touching lives and making a world of difference.

At this juncture, as our paths momentarily diverge, I want to extend my deepest gratitude for your trust and engagement. It's no small feat to embark on this profound journey of self-reflection and transformation. Your dedication to understanding, healing, and evolving is a testament to the resilient spirit that lies within you. Your commitment resonates deeply with me, and I cherish the moments we've shared through these pages. Remember, this book might be a guide, but the real change-maker, the hero of this story, has always been you.

Now, as I leave you to craft your narrative, I impart this thought:

In the orchestra of life, every note, no matter how fleeting or profound, has its place. Your song, with its unique rhythm and melody, adds to the symphony's richness. So, play it with gusto, dance to its tune, and let the world revel in your music.

Here's to transcending labels and scaling summits. Here's to you.

Emily Clark

A Personal Request from the Author

As a self-published author, your feedback means the world to me. Hearing from readers like you not only helps me grow as a writer but also helps other people find this resource when they need it most. If you found "From Family Scapegoat to Summit" helpful, I would be incredibly grateful if you could take a few moments to leave an honest review on Amazon. Your words could guide other people to the support and strategies they need to empower themselves to rise. Your voice truly matters and can make a difference in the lives of other people. Thank you from the bottom of my heart for your support and for joining me on this journey. Together, we are building a community of individuals freed from the grasp of family scapegoating, fostering healthier and more harmonious personal relationships.

Scan to leave an honest review

ABOUT THE AUTHOR

Emily Clark brings over two decades of expertise in understanding the complexities of family dynamics and the detrimental effects of emotional abuse. Emily's lifelong commitment has been to champion the healing journeys of those marginalized and misunderstood within their own families.

"From Family Scapegoat to Summit" comes as a testament to her dedication in providing solace and empowerment to those who have been unfairly labeled and burdened by familial expectations.

This book builds upon the success of her acclaimed "The Phoenix Path: Rising from the Ashes of Narcissistic Abuse", offering fresh insights and strategies tailored to those navigating the trials of the family scapegoat role.

With a unique blend of evidence-based methodologies and heartfelt understanding, Emily crafts a safe space for readers to reflect, heal, and grow. Through her prominent therapy practice, coupled with workshops and seminars, she continues her quest to enlighten and educate on the nuances of emotional trauma, its recovery, and the path to genuine self-love.

amazon.com/author/emily-clark

Unlock Your Full Healing Potential

Have you just completed Emily's transformative journey through "From Family Scapegoat to Summit"? Feeling inspired and ready for actionable steps? Look no further!

🌟 Dive Deeper with Our Exclusive Course!

Introducing: "From Family Scapegoat to Summit: A Transformative Journey to Healing and Empowerment"

- 💼 Hands-on, actionable lessons.
- 🤝 Engage with a supportive community of fellow journeyers.
- 🌱 Reclaim your legacy with group discussions, guided exercises, and more!

> "The synergy between Emily's book and this online course is unparalleled. It made my healing journey tangible" – Sarah T.

✨ LIMITED TIME OFFER ✨

As a reader of Emily's profound book, you are exclusively eligible for a special offer!

Get $50 OFF when you enroll in the course using the coupon code below:

🔗 Ready to Transform?

Visit Our Link:
https://payhip.com/b/38rAY

OR scan the QR code below

Don't just read about change — embrace it! Continue your journey with Emily and our supportive community today.

Made in United States
Orlando, FL
23 February 2024

44040466R00126